AuSSiE CHRiSTMaS BooK

Graeme

Mike, Marlyn
Shanae
love
Marco
&
LISA
xxx

Andrew Daddo ☆ Terry Denton

THaT AuSSiE CHRiSTMaS BooK

SCHOLASTIC
SYDNEY AUCKLAND NEW YORK TORONTO LONDON MEXICO CITY
NEW DELHI HONG KONG BUENOS AIRES PUERTO RICO

Scholastic Australia
345 Pacific Highway
Lindfield NSW 2070
an imprint of Scholastic Australia Pty Limited (ABN 11 000 614 577)
PO Box 579
Gosford NSW 2250
www.scholastic.com.au

Part of the Scholastic Group
Sydney • Auckland • New York • Toronto • London • Mexico City
• New Delhi • Hong Kong • Buenos Aires • Puerto Rico

First published by Scholastic Australia in 2007.
Text copyright © Andrew Daddo, 2007.
Illustrations copyright © Terry Denton, 2007.

Published in association with Mark Macleod and Selwa Anthony

National Library of Australia Cataloguing-in-Publication entry
Daddo, Andrew.
    That aussie christmas book.
    For children.
    ISBN 978-1-74169-043-9 (pbk.).
    1. Christmas stories, Australian. I. Denton, Terry, 1950- . II. Title.
A823.4

Typeset in Electra LH.

Printed in Australia by McPherson's Printing Group, Victoria.

10 9 8 7 6 5 4 3 2   08 09 10 11

For Mum, Dad, Bindy, Cam, Jub and Loch.
Thanks for my 40 Christmases – Andrew

For my 4 brothers and 40 years of rotten
presents – Terry

CONTENTS

CANDLES FOR CHRISTMAS

This is pretty much a true story.

I probably shouldn't tell you that. Now I have told you, though, I should at least change the names to protect the innocent (or the guilty).

I don't think the real people in this story would like you to know some things about them. Like the time one of them had diarrhoea, but didn't know it. Dio can be a bit like that, you know. It sneaks up on you, just like it did to this brother of mine. He was at a pool in his sluggos and he farted – only it wasn't just a fart; it was a fart with substance.

(Not just disgusting, but truly disgusting. We're talking – ah – follow-through here. I'm guessing this is not the time to get Terry to do a cartoon. Is it, Terry? Oh, Terry! You shouldn't have!)

So do you know what my bro did? He dived into the hotel pool, cleaned himself up, then went home and pretended it never happened.

Totally off, I know. And completely untrue. It was me, actually. Just kidding. It wasn't me. And it wasn't this brother of mine, either. But even if it was him, you wouldn't know which one it was, because I'm not using the real names. Everyone's protected – got it? Good.

I could let you in on the time he nicked a Fizz Wizz from the shop down the road and got nailed by the nasty old shopkeeper. His name was Simon, but he had a lisp, so he said his name was 'Thimon'. And Thimon thaid to him in that funny Scottish accent with all those rolling 'r's, 'Rrrrright, laddie! Eye wunt yew to goooo hoooome and tull ya mutherrrr what yuv dun hee-ya tuday.'

And when he got home, he actually told her. Duh! Who'd do that? Who'd dob on themselves? My brother, that's who.

And that is a true story.

Look, I just can't tell you which brother. If this brother of mine did find out I'd written a basically true story and told you these things about him, he'd probably get really aggro, come round to my house and try to bash me up – a completely ridiculous idea, because he knows he'd lose, even though he's had two real fights since Year 5 and I've only had one. Mine was in Year 6; he had one when he was in Year 7 against some guy who called him a mummy's boy and the other when he was nineteen. So yeah – he's got a bit more experience and he might win. But I reckon I could outrun him if it came to that, and if I couldn't, I'd back myself at begging for mercy.

So this is a story about him and it's true. Mostly. Maybe you can figure out the bits that aren't.

It was Christmas, a long time ago.

I think it was the year I got a Big Jim Hobie Cat from Father Christmas. Does that give you any idea how long ago it might have been? No? Well, it was back when there was a Big Jim. And Big Jim wasn't a doll; he was a god. And an action figure. And he was very *very* cool – except for his hair, which was plastic. GI Joe had the best hair. It was felt. We dug GI Joe, too. But this Christmas was all about Big Jim – for me, anyway.

For this brother of mine, Christmas wasn't about much at all. At least that was what he thought.

He got out of bed long before the sun was up to see what Father Christmas had brought him. The family down the road was a Santa Claus family. They used to talk about what Santa brought them. We talked about Father Christmas. Dad called him 'FX' for short. Pretty cool, my dad.

I was already camped out at Mum and Dad's door, waiting for any sign or sound of movement so my pretty cool dad got on with putting my Big Jim Hobie together. Another brother was trying to ride up and down the hall on his Toltoys skateboard (but they go crap on carpet) and my sister was sneaking a smoke in the paddock, while she pretended to feed the horse. She was always doing that.

My third brother was pounding his brand new PolyArmour Duncan Fearnley cricket bat with a rubber mallet. That was what we had to do in the old days with cricket bats. Pounding made them better, because the wood was all squashed together so the bat was denser and had a better 'meat'. If you're a cricket head you'll know exactly what I'm on about; if not, don't sweat it. I won't bring it up again.

Now, this first brother – the one the story is or isn't about – was sitting on his bedroom floor with his FX pillowcase turned inside out. He was looking for something he expected to be there, but wasn't. I don't think it'd be unfair to say he was in a mild state of shock. He'd been good for at least a week.

FX had dudded him in a major way. There was a book by Enid Blyton. Not Yay! There was a packet of snakes. Okay Yay! A surfing magazine. Pretty Yay! And two candles. Absolutely no way Yay!

That was it.

He visited all the other kids in our family, checked out what they had and went from a mild case of shock to curling up into a little ball at the end of his bed, sucking his thumb, pulling an ear and singing 'Mary had a little lamb'. It had been his favourite song when he was a baby – no one knows why. But his bed-ted wasn't a sheep; it was a rubber rottweiler he called Benji. Work that one out.

One of my other brothers lured me away from Mum and Dad's door to play Freddy Truman's Test Match. It's definitely the best cricket game ever invented – maybe the best game ever invented, but only if you dig cricket. And this was the original version with the weighted bat and the string. You can find it on ebay, but you have to be very lucky. It's still the best. Anyway, this brother was being Australia, I was the West Indies (it was when the West Indies were good at cricket) and we were right in the middle of a five-day test.

We said we were at the MCG.

It was all going well until he said I snicked a ball that was caught by the keeper. I said I didn't; he said I did. We had a fight. My sister came back from the horse trough, stinking of smokes, and told us to shut up or we'd wake Mum and Dad. That didn't sound like a bad idea. They could break up the fight.

My first brother came out of his coma of sadness and said, 'Are you sure that game's yours? All I got's a surf mag, a stupid book, some snakes – which I've already eaten – and two candles. I know I haven't had a very good year, getting caught stealing from the shop up the street and everything, but I didn't think old FX'd go that hard on me. Besides, the game says it's 'for 7+' and I'm closer to seven than you, so I think it might be mine. In fact, I bet you took it out of my Father Christmas pillowcase.'

'What?' My brother – the one who accused me of cheating at Test Match – and I said it at exactly the same time in exactly the same way.

'That game is mine, isn't it! You came into my room and nicked it out of my Father Christmas pillowcase. It's my game. Now GIVE IT BACK!' His eyes spun round so all we could see were the whites. He was mad. He'd lost it completely – just like when he had Coca Cola for the first time at the Murphys' house. The sugar sent him psycho.

He grabbed at the game, but my other brother pushed him to the side. So instead of getting the whole thing, he only got an edge. Test Match was a game played on a felt field, but he had enough of it to flip all the fielders. I grabbed a different part of the field and my other brother grabbed a piece too.

Then it was on. A three-way tug-of-war until the West Indies (me) and Australia (my other brother) pulled together against – you guessed it – England. For once, the Poms were pretty strong. He pulled; we pulled. Everyone was yelling and then the field tore all the way from one side to the other: from cover to mid-wicket.

That was when the yelling really started. And Dad came in and yelled louder than all of us. 'WHAT'S GOING ON?'

My brother (Australia) and I yelled, 'He ripped the field in half!' at the same time. But England yelled, 'They stole that game out of my Father Christmas pillowcase.'

'ONE AT A TIME!' Dad roared. Not so cool now, Dad, I thought – but, then, it was six o'clock in the morning.

'He,' said England, pointing at Australia, 'he stole that out of my Christmas pillowcase!'

'No, he didn't,' said Dad. 'It was in his pillowcase.'

'See!' Australia got all smarmy.

'Yeah, see!' I said.

'Yeah. See?' Dad was a parrot. 'Now go to bed and be quiet! We'll sticky tape the pitch up in the morning.' We could tell he was trying not to be cranky, but his eyes were all puffy and his voice croaked. He was cranky.

'It *is* morning,' said Australia, but Dad didn't hear.

When Dad was halfway down the hall, England whined, 'How do you know?'

'Wha –' said Dad.

'Well, Dad. How come you know it was in his pillowcase and not mine? If Father Christmas put it there, how would you know?'

'Yeah,' Australia and I said.

'Unless –'

'Unless nothing, you little smart mouth. I just do. It's a dad thing. Now-go-back-to-bed!' And now he wasn't even pretending not to be cranky. That was the last we saw of him until the real morning, when the sun was up.

Australia and I played until we were given the okay to be awake. We almost made it through five test matches.

England sat in his bed and stewed. Then he went to the kitchen and got some matches to light his candles. He discovered this was kind of pointless, because his candles were so slack they didn't even have wicks. Then he went back to the kitchen to get a knife so he could dig around in the wax for them. He figured that if he could fire the candles up, at least that'd be fun.

It took him about five minutes to obliterate both candles and discover that neither of them had a wick. They couldn't be lit at all. Christmas was going from bad to worse for him and the sun had barely cracked the horizon.

Sucked in.

Not much later, things took a genuine turn for the worse. Mum and Dad were into their second cup of tea and the rest of us were hanging out on their bed, telling them what Father Christmas had brought us.

'And what about you, Sunny Jim?' Mum said to my dudded brother, but that was what she and Dad called all of us.

'Oh, you know,' he said.

She kind of choked on a mouthful of tea and spluttered, 'How would I know?'

'I didn't mean you'd really know. I was just saying,

"you know," you know? It's like saying "it's like," you know? Besides, there's no way you would know what I got from Father Christmas, unless –'

'Unless nothing. Now what'd you get?' she snipped.

'Nothing.'

'Oh, don't be like that. It's Christmas Day; not sulking day. What was inside your pillowcase?'

'I'm serious. Nothing – pretty much. A stupid book by Enid Blyton.' He stuck two fingers down his throat as if he was trying to make himself spew. 'A surfing magazine and some other stuff.'

'Yeah?' said Dad. 'What was the other stuff?'

'Candles.'

The rest of us broke up. 'Candles?' Hardee hardee har har! 'You got candles? Father Christmas must hate your guts.' We pointed and laughed at him. Even Mum and Dad shared a sly look and a giggle.

Then he dissolved like the headache tablets my dad used to sell. He started bawling. The only thing that rivalled the flow of tears from his eyes was the river of dribble from his big sloppy lips. It was hard to understand much of what he said at first. Later, though, when the rest of us talked about it – when he wasn't around – we all agreed we were pretty sure he said, 'Why does Father Christmas hate me?' But it came out as 'hay-ay-ay-ay-ayte me'.

Then we all packed up laughing again. And for about four years we teased him by saying it back to him on Christmas morning. We weren't always nice to each other.

Dad booted the rest of us off their bed and out of their room, while Mum gave my brother a cuddle. 'He doesn't hate you, honey. I promise. Father Christmas doesn't hate you at all. In fact – ' But I couldn't hear any more.

We gobbled down breakfast, tried the TV, but turned it off, because as much as we wanted to like all that church stuff on every channel, it wasn't happening. Then we hung round the Christmas tree, hoping to see our names on the tags of the biggest presents.

Half the curtains in the good living room were closed.

We thought we might try the new cricket bat outside on the backyard pitch. 'Noooooooooo!' said Dad in slow motion. It was like he was at that bad part of the movie where everything goes wrong. The action star in ripped singlet with a bleeding cut over one eye (why don't they ever have a bleeding nose?) yells "noooooooooo!". Only Dad wasn't all beaten up. He was just Dad in his dark blue dressing gown with the big red Japanese dragon on the back.

But it stopped us.

'No going outside!' he barked. 'At least, not until after the tree presents.'

'Is there something hidden outside?' I had to know. It was probably for me, or my brother with the bat. Maybe for both of us. 'Is it for me? Or for us? Is it big? Can we ride it? Is it a bike? Two bikes? Last year you gave our sister a bike. Is it our turn? Is it our turn?'

'Stop it!' Dad looked at the ceiling, so we did, too. He often looked up there, but if he ever saw anything, we couldn't see it.

Mum came into the kitchen and my brother England had stopped crying. He looked happy now. I couldn't tell if he'd been given a lolly or something like that, but he was looking at the presents under the tree with hungry eyes. So maybe he'd been promised something big.

'How about we get started?' said Dad.

Everyone nodded.

'Where's your sister?'

'Giving the horse a Christmas carrot.' One of us smirked.

'Sometimes I think she loves that horse more than life itself.' Dad stuck his head out the kitchen window and shouted at the paddock. 'Horse Girl! We're doing presents.'

'Coming!' The word was muffled and followed by a bit of a cough. When she came in a lifetime later, she smelt of smoke and toothpaste and said the neighbours were burning all their wrapping paper already. 'How come it always takes so long for us to do presents?'

This time both Mum and Dad looked at the ceiling.

'Okay, Sunny Jim, get those candles FX gave you. I'll show you how to work them.'

'Oh, duh, Dad! Who doesn't know how to use candles?'

'Just get 'em.'

'Can't,' said my brother.

'Why?' Dad didn't look impressed.

'I chucked them.'

'What?' Mum and Dad said it together.

'Well, I dug around in them to find a wick, but there wasn't any. So I chucked them in next door's pool to see if they'd float. And guess what? They do. Anyway, they wouldn't work without a wick. I'm not an idiot, you know.'

'Clearly.' Mum looked at Dad when she said it, and added, 'What's worse than an idiot?'

Dad muttered something that only he understood.

Then, with a bit of an annoyed smile, he pulled the curtains back to reveal a brand new Shady Hollow surfboard. It was real fibreglass with a box fin, flyers, a swallowtail and starburst paint job. It was possibly the most beautiful thing I'd ever seen. 'Those weren't candles, you dill: they were surfboard wax. For your new – surfboard!'

Suddenly Dad was a game show host.

My brother looked dazed. 'Oh my god oh my god oh my god.'

'Yes, my son?' I couldn't help myself, but no one was listening to me.

'How did Father Christmas know to give me wax? Did he know what you were giving me? I feel like such an idiot.'

'It's like I told you: FX and I are pretty tight. I just gave him a call and said I was thinking about giving you a glass board and he said he'd look after the rest. He's a great guy.'

'Oh, Dad.'

'And Mum,' laughed Mum. 'It's from me, too.'

Talk about spewing! I don't think I've ever wanted

anything as badly as I wanted that surfboard. The others were spewing as well.

We went to Point Leo on the way to our cousin's place for Christmas lunch. It's a great surf beach. Dad stopped at a milk bar for some new wax. My brother ran down to the water with his new board, like a kid with money after Mr Whippy. He stayed in for ages. Talk about selfish. He even stood up on it. What a suck.

And what a hot board. I begged to have a go, and eventually Dad made him give me one. I couldn't stand up on it, though. The board wasn't as good as it looked. Then he let my other brother try it out.

He'd only had it for about five minutes when some moron on a windsurfer headed straight for him. And instead of ducking under the water or getting out of the way, my brother held the brand new Shady Hollow single fin up to protect himself.

The mong on the windsurfer didn't turn or anything. He plunged the nose of his board straight into the bottom of the brand new surfboard. The Christmas board. The windsurfer actually got stuck.

This was a disaster: as bad as anything that had ever happened to us. Maybe it was even worse than the time Dad was doing one-twenty up the highway and the truck zoomed past and peeled our boards straight off the roof of our car as if they were the top of a can.

My brother who'd dinged the board was sinbinned for the rest of the ride to our cousin's place. My brother who owned the board with the brand new ding finally stopped crying when our cousin said he could fix it. He's a boatie and smashes his catamaran up all the time. 'No worries,' he said. 'We've got fibre-glass and everything.'

We had Christmas lunch. We opened more presents. My sister went off to find a horse to feed. The world was a good place, again.

Then our cousin announced that the board was fixed and ready to go. He showed everyone how he'd done a 'bang-up job' on it. He was really proud of himself. 'No water's gonna get in there,' he said. He spun the board around and there, in the middle of the brand new board, was a big purple bruise.

It was gruesome. It was awful. My brother looked at his new board and started crying again.

But the rest of us didn't. Now his board looked exactly like ours.

How To

SABOTAGE

THE FAMILY CHRISTMAS

Family having too much fun?

It's all getting a bit too nice?

Everyone's saying, 'Oooh, I love it. Thank-you-thank-you!' Kissy-kissy sicky!

I know. It's happening all over town. Hey, want to leave your mark on Christmas this year?

Want to make this the Christmas everyone talks about in twenty years time?

Good one.

There are a few excellent things you can do – like hang different stuff on the tree – stuff that's off.

HEE! HEE!

You can swap the nametags on all the presents, put chilli powder in the gravy, leave the prawns out in the sun for a few hours, deflate the tyres on the family car so you don't have to go to Nanna's.

There are heaps of things.

You can even give your little brother a mohawk. That'll be cool. Besides, there's only six weeks between haircuts, so it's perfect timing for his first day at school and imagine the family photo. What a cack!

But have you thought about this?

Tell Mum you'll set the Christmas crackers at the table this year, but before you do, take out the lame jokes and crappy toys and replace them with some good, wholesome practical jokes. They're just jokes, and everyone loves a cracker joke, anyway. You'll save Christmas.

You'll be a legend.

Put these inside the crackers – just don't tell anyone I told you to. You're on your own, right?

Dog pooh – a wet slippery one will stink and you'll get caught. So have a hunt round the neighbourhood for a dry white one. We've all got someone living nearby who doesn't clean up after their dog. And the white ones are still disgusting: they just don't smell as bad. Your bogan cousin might think they're White Christmas and eat 'em.

A cow – yeah, I know. It'll be hard to fit it in there, but, mate, it'll be worth it.

Tinned spaghetti. Hold one end of the cracker and empty the whole tin in the other end. Just make sure that this one goes to the guest in the nice crisp white shirt.

Toilet paper with Vegemite or peanut butter on it. Whoever gets it will crap themselves, trust me!

Chunky soup – same deal as the spaghetti. If you choose the right brand, it'll look like spew. Or you could just use spew, but I don't know where you're going to get that from. You haven't had your Christmas dinner yet.

Grandma's green undies.

A python – you might have to seal the ends with rubber bands so he doesn't get out before the big moment.

Eyeballs – go to the butcher and ask him really nicely; he should have some that the science teacher hasn't picked up yet. Or maybe you could use cow guts or even a tongue. Yeah, use a tongue. Or sheep's brains. Totally disgusting.

Chewing gum – if you start saving your chewy now, by Christmas you'll have heaps. Hide it in your bedroom where your mum won't find it. Give it one last chew before you stick it in the cracker, so it's sticky. Maybe you can dribble honey on it. That'll be nice – and OFF!

A mouse – that's specially for Nanna! You can get it at the pet shop. A white one would be cute, but do you really want to be cute? Ahhhh, no! That's where we came in.

Good luck!

And don't forget to blame your big brother, the one who grunts a lot and smells like he ran a marathon two weeks ago, but forgot to shower. Everyone'll think it was him, anyway.

Incy Wincy Spider

Incy Wincy Spider saw Santa on the toot
and didn't want to scare him, so he hid under Santa's foot.
First he heard the thunder (*rrrrrrrrp!*),
but when he felt the rain (*phwoarrr!*)
Incy Wince got out of there and scrambled down the drain.

SMACKDOWN

Santa was distracted by a faint sound.

It might have been a tinkle, or a sprinkle. He knew he'd heard it before, but couldn't quite place it. Water maybe? Was that boy in the bed peeing himself?

Kind of off for a kid that age. Santa checked the kid. No, he was out cold. If he was making a puddle he'd be moving – maybe even going 'aahhh'. Santa went back to work.

There it was again. Now it was definitely more sprinkle than tinkle. It didn't sound as if this kid was waking up; he knew what that sounded like. It started with a rustling of sheets, and whenever Santa heard that, he knew he had about a minute to set the presents down and get out again. Most kids wriggled first, then stretched. Once they started grinding their teeth, though, he always knew it was time to go.

This wasn't any of those sounds, and yet it was strangely familiar. He squinted into the darkness. The kid was asleep. He was a big kid – maybe eight, but the size of a twelve-year-old. What did they feed them these days?

Then Santa saw a little light and suddenly knew exactly what the noise was and where it had come from; unconsciously, he ran his tongue over his teeth.

Perched on the rim of a glass of water beside the bed was the Tooth Fairy, wearing goggles and a snorkel. She was diving in to try and retrieve an eye-tooth. Those ones could be big and heavy and, if the kids didn't clean their teeth properly, very very slippery. That explained the noise. She was kicking the side of the glass as she worked her way down to the tooth. She hadn't even bothered to take her heels off. Sloppy, thought Santa, and noisy. He folded his arms and watched.

Clearly, this kid wasn't ever going to wake up. The Tooth Fairy had nailed him with sleep dust and he'd be done for at least an hour.

Santa cleared his throat. 'Uh-hmm!' The Tooth Fairy froze.

'What are you doing here?' said Santa. He didn't sound very Ho-Ho-Ho.

'I could ask you the same question, couldn't I?' Her voice was a bit squeaky.

'Ah, duh,' said Santa. 'Isn't that kind of obvious? Even a bug like you would know it's Christmas Eve.'

'Yeah, big deal. People lose teeth at Christmas too, you know. There's no need to make a song and dance about it.'

'Well, even if I did, they're my songs,' said Santa. 'I don't remember you having any, do I?' The Tooth Fairy glared at him. 'But I've got "Go, Santa, Go". There's "Santa Claus is Coming to Town". I like that one; it starts with bells. '*Ding ding ding ding ding ding* – Dashing through the snow, in a one horse open sleigh, o'er the hills we –'

'That's "Jingle Bells", you fat goose.'

'Right – nice to see you, too. Tooth Fairy.'

'Turn it up, Santa.' She tried to look annoyed.

'You don't like me very much.' He smiled. 'Do you?'

'Got that right.'

'Still upset about that time we went camping?'

The Tooth Fairy took a tiny two-dollar coin out of one front pocket and tossed it into the glass of water. It fizzed a bit and grew to the size of a normal coin. So that was how she did it! She sprinkled a bit of sparkle over the tooth she'd just fished out and watched it shrink in her hand. Then she stuffed it into her other front pocket. 'I hardly remember going camping with you at all, Fat Chops.'

To be fair, it had been a long time.

Back when they were best friends, Santa and the Tooth Fairy had gone camping in the desert. They set up their tent, snuggled down into their sleeping bags (Santa's was getting a bit more snug every year) and turned over to go to sleep.

But Santa had things on his mind and was soon awake again. 'Look up at the sky and tell me what you see,' he said suddenly.

The Tooth Fairy smiled dreamily. 'I see millions of stars.'

'Ho ho how right you are, my little friend. And what does that tell you?'

The Tooth Fairy waited a moment. 'Well, you big galosh,' she said. 'Astronomically speaking, it tells me that there are millions of galaxies and potentially billions of planets out there. Astrologically, it tells me that Mars is in Uranus. And chronologically, it must be about quarter past three in the morning.'

'Not bad for a fairy,' said Santa. 'Anything else?'

'Ah, let me see. Theologically, I suppose it says the Lord is all-powerful and we are small and insignificant. And, meteorologically, it looks as if we'll have a beautiful day tomorrow. I think that's about it. So when *you* look into a sky like this and see a million stars, what does that tell *you*?'

Santa was silent for a moment. He shook his large meaty head. 'Tooth Fairy, you little turkey, our tent has disappeared! I thought you said you'd hammer the pegs in!'

It wasn't being called a turkey that upset the Tooth Fairy; it was the 'little'. But how could Santa ever understand that? He was big. And not just big: he was massive. It also didn't help that the Tooth Fairy was copping all the blame for the tent disappearing.

Not fair.

Santa could have helped, but he'd grumped about being tired. And after the Christmas he'd had, he reckoned he deserved a decent snooze. That meant it had been up to the Tooth Fairy to get the pegs in properly and do everything else with the ground sheet and the ropes.

She'd kind of tried, but for goodness' sake, she was a fairy. And a she – and she did teeth, not pegs! Okay, so some idiots called teeth "toothy pegs". If she was the peg fairy or even the toothy peg fairy she'd understand Santa's blaming her, but, given that she was just the Tooth Fairy, she didn't understand why he'd got all sulky that the tent was gone.

She liked it even less when he moaned, 'You're going to have to get me a new tent, you little turkey. And exactly the same.'

'Fat chance,' she said. 'It's not as if you paid for it, anyway. You got it free for that gig you did at the camping goods store.'

Neither of them said much after that, although Santa did admit to himself that he probably could have helped with the pegs. Then he went back to sleep; it was kind of nice being under that blanket of stars, anyway.

But when he woke up, the Tooth Fairy was gone. They hadn't spoken since.

'So, are you still cranky about the "little turkey" line, or is it that you just don't like me anymore?'

'It's not that I don't like you; it's that I don't *get* you. Okay?'

Santa shook his head.

'Or not that I don't get *you*; I don't get the hype. Yeah? You work one day a year – one lousy day. Now, I'm big enough to admit that it's a pretty long day, but it is just one day – and you're, like, a superstar! You've got posters, you've got impersonators, fan cards, lollies, cakes, dress-ups. Everything. Anything. Movies. Kids write you letters. They don't even have to put a street address on the envelope and the mail still arrives at your place. It's psycho! And you work one day a year for it. One lousy day.'

The Tooth Fairy was getting herself all worked up. Her wings were flapping as she talked. 'And me? I work every day of every year and I get – what? Jack! That's what I get. And I'm jack of it! No one even knows what I look like. I'm a myth. Seriously. Ask any eight-year-old what the Tooth Fairy looks like and he'll say I've got a tooth for a head.'

Santa laughed. So that was the problem. She was jealous!

'It's not funny, you big fat elf! And you're as bad as the rest of them. You never write; you don't call.'

'Ho ho ho.' Santa tried to laugh it off. 'I can't keep up with your mobile number. Is it 0411, or 0412, or 3 or 4 or what? My emails kept bouncing because your mailbox was always full.' The Tooth Fairy sucked her perfect teeth. 'And I don't exactly see you around. It's not as if you turn up to Christmas parties, is it?'

'I don't get invited, big guy!'

'Okay, okay. Getting a bit personal here.'

'Getting under all that skin of yours? Well, good – because you've got enough of it! So, Santa, how does it feel to be the most famous fat man in the world?' She was sounding like a TV reporter. 'I bet when you stand on the scales a sign pops up saying, "One at a time, please". You were born with a silver shovel in your mouth. Hey, Santa, if you fell over, no one would laugh, but the ground would crack up. You with me on that one, big fella?'

Santa turned bright red. 'You stink, you little –'

'Don't blame me. It's the teeth that stink! And that's what I get for all the cash I put out.'

Santa rolled up one sleeve and then the other. 'No, little toothy pegs. Your attitude stinks. It's not my fault that everyone loves me. Get yourself a marketing director. Get an agent. Start small and build yourself up, do the shopping centre gigs – but don't blame me because your profile's down.'

'As if I'd be jealous of you! Red's so seventies – and fur? Keep up, you bogan!'

'Right! That's it. No one calls me a bogan. Let's get it on!'

'You? You're going to fight me – the Tooth Fairy?'

Santa nodded. 'I'll rip your little wings off and watch you run round in circles. Then I want to hurt you.' He put his giant fist into his sack and pulled out some boxing gloves. 'Sorry – ' He checked the gift tag. 'Tom Griffiths – I'm gonna borrow your present for a minute.'

The Tooth Fairy looked a bit edgy. 'That's not fair.'

'Good point,' he muttered. He dug back into his Santa sack, pulled out Boxer Barbie, ripped the packet open, took the gloves and threw them at the Tooth Fairy. 'Okay, now it's fair.'

The boy in the bed with the gap in his teeth rolled over.

'He's gonna wake up soon,' said the Tooth Fairy. 'In a minute – two, tops.'

'This won't take long,' said Santa. He started hopping from foot to foot as if he was a boxer warming up. The house shook, but the Tooth Fairy decided not to say a thing. 'In the red corner,' said Santa, 'weighing in at one hundereddd and ninety-ninnnnne pounds is Sant-aaaahhh Claus!' Then he made a crowd noise. 'Hoooooooarrrr! And in the pink corner,

weighing in at one-ah pound-ah, and about to be poundedddddd – is the little maggot otherwise known as the Tooth Fairy!' He made another crowd noise, but more restrained this time. 'So let's get ready to RUMBLE!'

'This is psycho,' said the Tooth Fairy.

Santa took a step forward and swung.

The Tooth Fairy ducked.

He missed. 'Damn right it's psycho. I should have sorted you out years ago. If you'd put the pegs in the ground properly when we went camping, I'd still have my tent.' He had another swing. Another miss.

The boy ground his teeth.

'Look!' said the Tooth Fairy. 'He's waking up!'

'Let him.' Another swing – and a miss. 'He can be

a witness to the day I took you out in the Christmas Smackdown.'

'You've been watching way too much wrestling on TV.'

'Shuddup, midget!' That punch almost connected. So did the next one. The Tooth Fairy was dodging shot after shot. Santa thumped round the bedroom, knocking things over and the boy really would wake up any minute. Fairy dust was good – but not that good.

The Tooth Fairy had to end it, or both their careers would be over. But how? She hovered in front of the big man and looked for an opening. He was all over the place. He wasn't a fighter. Anyone could see he had no idea how to look after himself.

The Tooth Fairy zipped to the left a bit, zapped a bit right and when Santa missed with a combination upper cut - right cross, she let him have it. A beauty – right in the chops!

'Ow! Crikey, that hurt!' yelled Santa. 'And you've knocked my tooth out!'

'Sorry Santa sorry Santa sorry Santa!' And the Tooth Fairy really was. Sorry for everything. Sorry for the fat jokes, sorry about the tent, and now she was really, really sorry, because she thought she'd finished for the night and – thanks to her gorgeous right cross that had taken out the big man's tooth – she had to fly all the way to the North Pole and wait for him to come home, eat something, go to bed, fall asleep and then sprinkle him and Mrs Claus with fairy dust so she could take his tooth and leave him the cash.

It was a nightmare. The night before Christmas.

The boy in the bed started to rub his eyes.

'He's up,' said the Tooth Fairy. 'Gotta fly!'

'Lucky for you, midget,' said Santa. 'I guess I'll see you at my place later, right?'

'Possibly.' She shrugged.

'And this time, can you pay me in North Pole currency?' Santa barked as he bolted up the chimney.

'And this time,' the Tooth Fairy squawked back, 'clean the tooth first. Even when you were a kid, your teeth were disgusting. Got a last-minute gift idea for you – give yourself a toothbrush this year.'

HAM AND PORKIES

The story of why we eat ham and pork at Christmas

Once upon a time there
were three little pigs.
Three chunky little pigs.
They were aspirational
pigs, who were good at
asking for things – like
building materials.

HEE!
HEE!

The first little pig
scabbed some straw to
build his house. (You
know what happens next.)

The second little
lardie was smarter than his
porky pal. He scrounged
some sticks to build his
house – and ended up like
the first little pig.

The third pig was
smarter than the other
two put together. He
talked the bricklayer
into giving him some
bricks. His house was
fabulous. The wolf
didn't even bother
trying to blow it down.

Smart wolf.

So things went well for little pig number three.
He got to do all sorts of home improvements.

He added a flat screen TV.
A microwave. Even a water
feature out the back.
At Christmas time, he
even put up lights.
But the big bad wolf
hadn't forgotten the third
little pig. And he was
hungry again. Really
hungry. 'Hey, little pig,' he said.

'Yeeeeeeeeeees, Mr Wolf,' said the little pig.

'Let me in, or I'll huff and I'll puff – ' (And then
it goes on a bit. Maybe the big bad wolf wasn't really
that smart.)

When the pig heard a noise on the roof, he knew it was the wolf. Had to be. So he set a massive pot under the chimney and started a roaring fire under it.

Of course, it wasn't the wolf at all. He'd blown himself out. No staying power.

It was Santa, who ended up *splat* in the pig's pot.

Not happy, little pig. Not happy at all.

So Santa climbed out of the pot, looked around and saw the third little pig.

'I thought you were someone else. Sorry, Santa,' said the little pig.

'You'll be sorry, all right,' said Santa. And he stuffed the pig in the pot, cooked him and ate him up. Absolutely delicious!

But Santa got terrible indigestion. (Too much ham can do it every time.)

So he said, 'I could go another round with a chunky little pig.' And he rubbed his tummy. 'But not just yet. Think I'll wait about a year.'

And that is the TRUE story of why we eat porkies at Christmas. (But it's not the only time we tell them!)

THAT'S SOME PIG !

It was Uncle Merlin's turn to have everyone for Christmas lunch.

Uncle Merlin is Mum's brother. He's a farmer and he's as psycho as his name. He only ever wears gumboots and shorts and a green shirt. I've never seen him in pants or a jumper – not even when it's freezing.

Mum calls him 'Magic' and Dad calls him a goon – only behind his back, though. But Uncle Merlin reminds me of the Crocodile Hunter.

We left home after breakfast and got to his place before lunch. As we came through the gate Dad leant on the car horn.

Like the rest of the country, Uncle Merlin's place was pretty dry; there wasn't much grass around. Lots of dust, though. He had cut a bunch of tyres in half, painted them white and planted them in two rows. That was the only way visitors would know where his driveway was and his front yard wasn't.

Before we got anywhere near the house, he was at the front steps – with shorts, a green shirt on and a giant dog by his side. At least, I thought it was dog. He had a dog collar on and my uncle was holding a lead.

The beast was massive, but partly hidden by my uncle's legs.

I had another look. It wasn't a dog; it was a pig – a big brown pig with three legs. But I'll get to that in a minute. When we climbed out of the car, the pig came forward, as if it was saying g'day.

'Merry Christmas, Magic,' said Mum, trying to scoot round the snorter and give Uncle Merlin a kiss. What are you doing with that pig in the house?'

Dad cacked. 'Finally get yaself a girlfriend, did ya?'

'Good one,' said Uncle Merlin. I'd forgotten how slowly he spoke. 'And, no-ope, I ain't got a girlfriend, new or old. It's a pig – and not just any pig. This is some pig. It's the kinda pig that has to be looked after.' He grinned at us, then the pig, then at us again. 'A pig like this is too good to leave outside, believe me. You're gonna love him.'

We all looked. He seemed like an ordinary pig: ugly, snot coming out his nose, pink skin around his beady little eyes, hair like wire. Just plain ugly. And that was the world's biggest dog collar pressing into his fat neck.

'Okay, what's so special about the pig?' said Mum. 'Apart from the fact that it's missing a leg and it lives in your house?'

'Don't laugh, right?'

Dad put his hands up and started to back away from the pig. 'I was just kidding about this being your girlfriend, Merl.'

'Wow. Same joke, different target and still not funny. You're on fire. But we were talking about the pig. He's special. He can count.'

'Oh yeah?'

'Yeah!'

'Hey, pig,' I said. 'What's two plus two?'

The pig looked at Uncle Merlin, then at us, and he stomped on the ground three times.

'That's one plus two, pig. I said *two* plus two.'

The pig rapped out four stomps.

'Some pig,' said Mum.

Uncle Merlin was right into it. He gave the pig a kiss and everything. 'He can draw, too, watch this. Pig –' And now Uncle Merlin was using his big hey-cows-come-and-get-ya-dinner voice. 'Pig, draw a face.'

The pig sort of scooted a bit with its pink snout in the ground. There was a mess of snorting and squealing as he seemed to go round and round in circles – almost as if he were a dog looking for a place to sleep.

When the pig backed off and the dust had settled, there was a face in the dirt. It wasn't much of a face – just a big circle with a line for a mouth, another one for the nose and two snout marks for eyes. But it was a face. We could all see that. And the hoof marks made it look as if it had freckles.

'How'd you know he could do this stuff, Magic?' said Mum.

Uncle Merlin just nodded. 'He can talk, too.'

'It was fun while it lasted, Merlin. But now you've lost it.' Mum snorted like a pig. 'Pigs can't speak. They can fly, sometimes. But they definitely can't speak.'

That made him laugh. Really laugh. We all laughed. I think the pig did, too. And then Uncle

Merlin said, 'How you going, pig?'

And the pig snorted. It sounded like "okay". Really.

'How you going again?' laughed Uncle Merlin.

And the pig snorted and once more it sounded like "okay".

My little brother, who'd gone to do a wiz on the electric fence as soon as he got out of the car, suddenly turned up. 'Hey,' he said. 'It sounded like that three-legged pig just said "okay".'

Uncle Merlin nodded. 'That's exactly what the pig said.' He looked proud enough to burst. 'I told your mum and dad he could speak.'

'That sure is some pig,' said Dad, sounding as if he believed himself. 'So why's he only got three legs?'

'Well, ain't that obvious? You don't eat a pig that good all at once.'

AUNTIE CHERYL

Oh, the pain, the irreversible misery of picking up the phone when it rings on Christmas Day.

What were you thinking? Clearly, you weren't. You were in such a feeding frenzy of presents that you acted like the phone was another present and you had to have it.

Idiot! Lunatic!

And now you're stuck on the phone with some old Auntie Cheryl – only she's not stuck on the phone with you, because she loves talking to you. To anyone, really. She's the auntie who lives alone, and now that she's got hold of you she's never, ever going to let you go.

Worse than that, you can see your little brother and sister in the other room picking through your brand new toys. Christmas has turned bad, very bad.

Although it isn't really your fault. Anyone could have ended up stuck with Auntie Cheryl. The old phone's ringing its head off and you're closest to it, so what do you do? Of course you pick up and shout, 'Merry Christmas!' before your mouth is anywhere near it. And when you finally get the receiver to your head, there's nothing. Just a croaky breathing that sounds a bit flat and sad. 'Hello?' you say, still thinking there's a present in there somewhere. 'Merry Christmas?'

The croak finds a voice that's really just a bigger croak. 'Oh, you are home. I didn't know if you'd be there. I was just going to leave a message. I was. Yes. If you want, I can still leave a message. I don't want to be any trouble. You'll have to hang up and don't answer when I call back. That's a bit silly, though, now that you're there. Hello, dear. It's your old Auntie Cheryl.' She coughs it down the line. 'Merry Christmas to you, too. My beautiful niece.'

You laugh; it's kind of funny because you're not her niece. If you were anything you'd be her nephew, because you're a boy. But then, you don't really know how you're related to this woman on the other end of the phone who's holding up your Christmas morning. You think your dad's related to her, but you don't know how.

In fact, if you thought about it for long, you don't really remember her at all.

And, watching your little sister as she starts tearing into the paper on your second last present, you don't even care. 'Hey!' you yell into the phone – but not at Auntie Cheryl; at your sister. If she hears you, she doesn't look up or stop opening your present.

'Hey!' you shout again.

Then Auntie Cheryl says, 'Sorry, dear. I should have put my teeth in before I called. Hang on a sec.' There's a rattling, sucking kind of sound. 'Is that better?' It is. You can't believe that she actually called without sticking her teeth in. 'Age is a curse, you know. Look after your teeth, dear, or they won't look after you.'

You'll think about that later. You're watching your dad help your sister unwrap your present and they're both smiling at you in a weird way, to make it clear that they know something you don't. 'Hey! That's mine!' You try again.

Your dad waves his hand in a way that could be come-here or go-away, but is really get-that-phone-back-to-your-head-it's-rude-not-to-answer-when-someone-is-talking-to-you.

Any minute, you're going to lose it. If you were on the walk-around phone, you'd go over and rip your present out of their hands. But you're on the phone your mum said was a steal at that garage sale for fifty bucks. It's a fake old-fashioned wall one with the short cord to the bit you stick next to your ear. It's such a pain to use!

'Are you there, my favourite niece? I've got a special present for you.'

'Yeah, I'm here.' You're trying not to sound aggro. That'd be pretty rude. And now that she's mentioned presents –

'I'd understand if you weren't, of course,' she says. 'I wouldn't expect you to give up all this time to me on Christmas Day, because I know you're so busy with everything else. That's why you're my favourite niece.'

And then you say, 'But I'm not your niece, Auntie Cheryl. I'm your nephew. It's me, Ha – '

'Oh, my God! Of course you're not a girl. I'm so embarrassed. Did I say old age is a curse? It's not just your teeth that fall out; it's your memory as well. But I do remember when I was a girl – not a silly old thing like I am now – I had a bit of a deep voice, too. Just like you, dear. And then once I started smoking it got deeper and deeper, like a swimming pool when you walk into it from the shallow end. You know?'

You stop listening, because it's starting to sound a lot like one of Grandma's stories about the good old days that go on forever. You pull the receiver away from your head and glare as your dad and sister peek inside the paper and then back at you.

'Talk!' Your dad mouths the word and nods.

You shake your head.

He glares at you, as if you're a golf ball that won't go into the hole – the kind of ball that makes him extremely angry. You clamp the receiver back to your ear, Auntie Cheryl's still talking. She's up to the bit where she starts coughing uncontrollably. Or is that laughing? Maybe she's smoking. So you pull the receiver away again and your dad mouths, 'So rude! It's CHRISTMAS!'

When you put the receiver back to your ear once more, there's a sound that's exactly like water running. You look at the kitchen sink, but the tap's not on. Then there's the sound of a toilet flushing. 'Is that a toilet flushing?' you say.

'Oh, sorry, dear. I didn't think you'd hear that.'

You hold the receiver away from your ear again, scared of what you might hear next.

'Last chance!' Your dad actually growls while he points. He even gets up off the floor and comes over to you. Your little sister looks as if she's been abandoned. She'll start crying any minute. She's such a two-year-old. 'Who is it?' your dad whispers finally.

'It's your auntie,' you say.

'Yes, dear?' says Auntie Cheryl.

'Nothing,' you say.

Dad looks at you as if you've lost it. 'Which one?'

You make that face you see all the time on American TV shows, when the actors pucker their lips, smile and frown all at the same time. It's like saying,

"Duh, you loser" without actually using the words. That would be a big mistake, saying that to your dad. But making a face that says it is okay, because he might think it's a face that says something else.

'And what are you all doing on this fine Christmas Day?' comes the croak again.

'What are we doing today?' you whisper to Dad.

He makes the same face you made at him. So he definitely doesn't think it means you're a loser. 'Everyone's coming over here for Christmas lunch.' He whispers it, but Auntie Cheryl hears him anyway.

'That sounds nice, dear,' she says. 'It's important to have the family together for Christmas.'

Why don't old ladies ever have anything wrong with their hearing? Grandma hears everything – even stuff that people have only thought!

'Yes, family is important.' You repeat it, because it sounds like the right thing to say and your dad's still hanging around you like a bad fart – only now, he's mouthing, 'I'm not here, I'm not here.' You pull that "loser" face so hard it makes you look like a duck and he goes back to the abandoned little sister still tearing at the paper on your present. Thank God for thick wrapping paper and lots of sticky tape, you think.

Cool. Now you can blow Auntie Cheryl off the

phone. 'Yeah, anyway. It's pretty mad here, so I'd better go.'

Then she says something that makes you listen. 'I'm going to be alone for Christmas, but that's okay. Isn't it?'

'That sucks.'

Dad's suddenly back. It sucks that he hates the word 'sucks'. He's banned it. You knew it'd cost you pocket money if he or Mum heard you using it, but you thought you were safe. It sucks that they've got good ears, too.

You try to make it right. You need all the pocket money you can get, because it looks as if no one's given you that remote control car you were after. Then you get a mad idea. 'You should come here for Christmas.'

Silence. From both Auntie Cheryl and Dad.

Then they both speak at once.

'Who is it?' says Dad.

'I don't think I could,' says Auntie Cheryl.

'Of course you could,' you say.

'Well, I suppose I could, couldn't I? Do you think I should, though?'

'Who the hell is it again?' Dad's looking quite stressed.

'Of course you should come to our Christmas Day. You're our auntie, and that makes you part of the family. You should definitely come. Especially if you're bringing money or a remote control car.' Dad looks ready to pop. 'Kidding, just kidding,' you say. 'You don't have to bring anything if you don't want to. Just bring yourself.' That's what your mum says to everyone who's coming and rings first to ask if they should bring something.

'You might be in luck,' says Auntie Cheryl. 'I was taught that if you wish hard enough, anything can happen. Have you been wishing?'

'I'm gonna start right now,' you say.

'Good girl,' she croaks. 'And I'll bring some biscuits. What time should I get there?'

'Dunno,' you say. 'Now, I spose. See ya!'

'Merry Christmas,' you hear her say as the receiver goes back to the old-fashioned cradle.

'Who the hell was that? Who have you asked for Christmas lunch?'

'I told you. Your auntie.'

'Which auntie?'

'The one who talks on the phone while she goes to the toilet.'

It's Dad's turn to look psycho. That'll teach him to tool around with your presents. 'What?'

'The auntie with the deep voice. The one that smokes. Auntie – '

'Auntie who?' He's steaming up.

'Auntie Cheryl.'

'We haven't got an Auntie Cheryl.'

'We do now,' you say. 'And she's bringing me a remote control car for Christmas.'

Incy Wincy Spider

Incy Wincy Spider climbed up the Christmas tree.
When he saw old Santa, he jumped up on his knee.
Santa barely noticed, but when he did he cried,
'You scared me half to death, you bug. Now it's time you died!'
Whack!

JOKES FROM MANLY WEST
(THE BEST!)

What sort of pies fly?
Magpies

What's Santa's favourite drink?
Fanta

Why didn't Santa deliver all the presents?
He got stuck in a chimney.

What is the most dangerous thing at Christmas?
Santa Claws.

Why is Santa so fat?
Because he eats too much.

When does Santa deliver gifts?
In the present.

What do you call a Christmas joke?
A cracker! Or a croak.

Why did the one-armed Santa cross the road?
He wanted to get to the second hand shop.

Why didn't Santa's skeleton cross the road?
He didn't have the guts.

Why does Santa have three gardens?
So he can go Hoe Hoe Hoe.

What goes Oh Oh Oh?
Santa walking backwards.

What goes Ho Ho Ho Clunk?
Santa laughing his head off.

Why did the Irishman take a toilet to the snow?
To bog in.

Why wasn't Rudolph's nose glowing?
It was daytime.

Who is Santa's friskiest reindeer?
Prancer.

Why are Christmas trees green?
They're sick.

Why does Santa fly?
Because he can't afford the petrol to drive.

What do you call a fake Santa?
Imposter Claus.

What do you call a deer in a storm?
A rain-deer.

What do you say if Santa's calling the roll?
'Present!'

Why did the Chinese sailor desert his ship?
He was sick of junk food.

Knock Knock
Who's there?
Rain.
Rain who?
It's rain, dear – and you're getting wet.

Knock Knock
Who's there?
Santa
Santa Who?
Not Santa *Who* – Santa *Claus!*

Where do Santa's helpers
keep the presents?
On the (Shhh!)elf.

What's Santa's wife's secret?
She's got Claws.

Mrs Claus was standing out the front of their place with an armload of hay. Santa was reading the paper inside.
Mrs Claus: Where's the reindeer?
Santa: In the sky – where else would it be?

What do you call a smelly Santa?
Farter Christmas.

Knock Knock
Who's there?
Rude
Rude who?
Rudolph the red-nosed reindeer.

Who is Santa's rudest reindeer?
Rudolph.

Knock Knock
Who's there?
Polly.
Polly who?
Polly ate some holly

Knock Knock
Who's there?
Police
Police who?
Police, let me in – I'm Father Christmas.

Who is never hungry at Christmas?
The turkey – it's always stuffed.

What do you say to a stressed-out snowman?
Chill out!

What kind of turkey can't fly?
A Christmas turkey.

Who is Santa's fastest reindeer?
Dasher.

If Minnehaha married Santa Claus, what would her name be?
Minnehohoho.

Knock Knock
Who's there?
Mary.
Mary who?
Mary Christmas.

Who is the most grace-
ful reindeer?
Dancer.

What is red, black and
white and comes down your chimney?
Santa covered in soot.

What did Mrs Claus say when
Rudolph predicted the weather?
Rudolph the red knows rain, dear.

Why are there twenty-five letters
in the alphabet at Christmas time?
Because the angels sang No-El.

SNOOPATHON

What I so totally love about Christmas is that every cool present in the house is mine.

I'm like the only one who gets cool presents. There's just me. And Mum and Dad. Well – we're like the only people. We've got a dog called Pup, a goldfish called Nemo (duh!) and a lorikeet. We found him as a baby, but haven't managed to set him free – yet.

But we will. Fluffy's beautiful.

We called him Fluffy because that's how he was when we found him – just like a puff of feathers sitting on the ground. The dog was the one who noticed him. It could have been really messy, but Mum was quick enough. She pushed Pup away just in time and put the baby bird in her hat.

'So cute,' Mum said.

'And fluffy,' I said.

'So that's what we'll call him. Fluffy.'

I wasn't sure. 'Fluffy' sounded like a grandma name for blowing off.

We bought birdseed from the shop on the way home, but Fluffy wouldn't eat it. We tried Weet-Bix, milk, porridge, toast with butter and without. Even sultanas. But Fluffy still wasn't interested.

Then I googled 'what to feed a bird you've found'. Somewhere in the list of like a gazillion answers was 'honey'. Fluff was into it; that was all he ate for ages. He got bigger and bigger. We had to get a proper cage instead of the one we'd found up the street on hard rubbish day. We started giving him other food, too. He loves Vegemite toast. Don't ask me why, but he does. And if he eats porridge, it has to have honey on it – not brown sugar.

Picky wicky Fluffy wuffy.

Then we had to buy an even bigger cage so he

could flap about a bit. He kind of started talking and he was more interesting than a fish. Fluffy was like part of the family, and it just seemed to get harder and harder to find the right day to let him go. We've tried, but some days are like too hot; others are too cold, okay. Once, when the weather was perfect and we really were going to set Fluffy free, I was sure I saw an eagle hanging around near the Milsons' place.

It was huge.

It wouldn't have been right to let Fluffy go.

The eagle would have eaten Fluffy. Then Fluffy would have been dead and we would have killed him and I so do not want to be called Lorikeet-murdering-Mandy-Davis for the rest of my life.

I'm not even sure I want to be called Mandy Davis.

Mandy Abbot, maybe. Or Amanda Abbot. When I get married to Calvin Abbot I'll probably want to change my name to Amanda, because I'll be grown up. That's what Mum did. She stopped being Fifi and turned into Fiona. It sounds nice, don't you think – Amanda Abbot? The only time it doesn't, is if I say it three times quickly. Amanda Abbot, Amanda Abbot, Amanda Abbot.

See? Amanda Rabbit. Or Oh, man, da rabbit. Ben Herbertson is like such a major stirrer, he'd be the one who'd call me 'The Man Rabbit'. He's the one who started calling Emily Bellamy 'Smellamy' and Richard Lorner 'The Canary', because he sings in a weak, high voice.

I'm tall and I've got big teeth, too. So 'The Man Rabbit'? Defo.

But maybe things won't work out with me and Calvin. That might be for the best, anyway. I've always thought I'd like to call my first son Roger, after my grandfather, because Mum called me Amanda after her grandfather. No, just kidding. It was Amanda, after her grandmother.

If I married Calvin and had a son – oh, see? Roger Rabbit.

I don't think so. It might be time to let things cool down a bit with Calvin Abbot before they go too far.

Okay, like before they even get started. Two hands up, thumbs together, pointers out. What-*ever!*

Mum said after the eagle tried to kill Fluffy – because he probably knew we were going to let him go that day – we all had to stop saying that we'd found Fluffy and start saying that Nanna gave him to us as a Christmas present and we'd had him for yonks. That's what she said: 'yonks'.

L is for *Loser!*

I said everyone knew we'd had Fluffy forever.

She said I talked too much.

That meant we were keeping Fluffy. Yay! Pretty much.

The only bad part about getting to keep Fluffy was that I didn't know if it counted as a real Christmas present, or a lie. And if it did count as a real Christmas present it meant I'd be a present down, which was completely jank – and that's bad, even though my dad thinks it sounds good. Being old must suck.

I had to find out what was going on with my presents, and that's how I ended up here.

Did I tell you I'm stuck?

I'm in the roof, mostly. But my feet are in the lounge room.

They're sticking through the ceiling. That's the good ceiling – the one made of pressed metal. This is the exact one that Mum went all gooey over, the first time she saw the house. Dad said it was like the reason she wanted to live here. And now my size eights are sticking through the middle of it.

Wouldn't you think if a ceiling was made of pressed metal it would be like strong enough to stand on?

Play that game-show noise now, okay babe! *Bump-oooowooooowooowooowooow!*

Of course, it wasn't really my fault that I went through the ceiling. It's my parents' fault. Obviously. If they'd hidden my presents in the usual places, I wouldn't be perched up here as if I was riding one of the beams in the roof.

Usually my presents are pretty easy to find. They put them in the top of their cupboard, or the boot of Dad's car. I've snooped round and found presents under their bed, in the laundry, in the linen press. One year they hid them in the oven, but that didn't go so well, because we had a cold snap and the heater had been put away, so I turned the oven on and stood in front of it to try and get warm.

Swimsuit Barbie didn't like the heat that summer.

This year, though, I looked and I couldn't find where they'd hidden them. Not one. There weren't even any presents for the cousins. Nothing. Mum always shops early. Sometimes she shops in the sales straight after Christmas and saves the stuff up for the next one. But the 2005 Boxing Day Crush finished her. She said 'never again'. (Why did all those dumb parents want a cheap TV anyway? In a year it'd be too old to watch.)

I'd been thinking the presents might be at Dad's work. But, then, they'd never tried to hide them there before.

The whole snoopathon had failed and I started to get worried. Things were like so not normal. Three weeks to Christmas, and you wouldn't have even known it! I went to bed and tried to figure out where my presents were.

Not in their cupboard. Not in the boot. Not in the laundry. Not in the –

That was when I heard the springs of the ladder being stretched. The roof! We've got one of those pull-down attic ladders. Dad fitted it himself, so it's a bit dodgy, but it works okay. Once it was in, he added a light and put plywood across the ceiling beams to make a floor. Then he loaded the space up with piles of stuff Mum had put aside for 'another day'.

I could hear whispering, so I knew there was a secret in the house. It had to be about my presents.

'Careful, careful!' That was Mum.

'Yeah, all right!' Dad. They would have been better talking normally. Dad's deep grumble's harder to understand than his loud whisper.

Sneaky. Why hadn't I thought of the roof? Duh! It had to be the new spot for the really good presents.

I was so excited I hardly slept. Snooping for presents is almost as good as actually getting them. It's like looking for buried treasure. Or Easter eggs. I know they're round the place somewhere – I just have to find them.

And now I kind of had.

I took a sickie from sport and rushed home. I'd have the place to myself for about an hour. Dad wouldn't be home for ages and Mum would get home about the same time I was supposed to. Her job was good like that.

I went straight for the attic ladder and winced at the noise of those springs as it came down from the ceiling. Even though I knew I was the only one around, the noise still made me feel as if I'd get busted any minute.

Up the steps. At the top I pulled the dangling cord to turn the light on, but it didn't work. Argh! Nothing works the way it's meant to in this place. I pulled it a few more times. Still nothing.

It was too dark to see much, so I climbed back down and went to the laundry for the torch.

Dead.

Batteries. Where were the stupid batteries? In the big laundry cupboard? Of course they were. 'A place for everything and everything in its place.' That was the saying on Mum's favourite teatowel.

I still had time to check the roof, so it was back up the ladder.

What a mess. This was obviously the place for everything that didn't have a place. All the stuff! Suitcases, golf clubs, camping gear, Tedalina (my old teddy).

Tedalina? But she'd been accidentally left at the old house when we moved and the new people were too nasty to give her back. That was what I'd been told. Dad said the minute we left the house the newbies had moved in. And when he went back to get poor Tedalina, they'd already done at least one run to the tip and couldn't remember seeing her anywhere.

I cried heaps. I always took Tedalina everywhere. She was my best friend. Mum and Dad said they were really sorry.

Yeah, right.

I picked Tedalina up and rubbed my nose against hers, just like I'd always done. She smelt pretty much the same. And she was smooth. And yum. And I don't know how I ever slept without her and I knew that now I'd never have to again. Double triple quadruple Yay!

I clutched Tedalina tight to my chest and pressed on through the junk. I said to myself if I found my old Bangie, Mum and Dad were really going to get it. It was bad enough when I lost my ted, but the day Bangie was taken by the Big Bad Bangie-stealing Bunny was one of the worst days of my life.

There were boxes of old photos. Boring old paperwork. Board games I hadn't thought about playing forever – but no presents.

Then there was a noise.

Kind of like a rattle, I guess. It came from deep in the roofspace (you couldn't really call it an attic), beyond where Dad had laid the plywood floor – where it was dark and you had to walk on the beams and avoid the fluffy pink stuff that kept the house kind of cool in summer and warm in winter. Batts. That's what they were.

I shone the torch into the darkness, but there was nothing to see.

Rattle rattle went the noise, but only when I shone the torch near the chimney. It might have been a coincidence. Maybe the noise was just the wind. But, then, the wind only whimpered in Dad's dumb stories. 'Oh, the whimpering wind,' he says. I walked to the very edge of the plywood floor and swept the light across it. 'Hello? Is anything there?'

There was a bigger rattle and a bigger squeaky sort of whimpery, hissy noise.

Something was definitely back there. And it was alive.

I was like oh-my-god! It was a puppy. Or a kitten. I couldn't believe it. I'd wanted to get another dog forever, but Dad was off the idea. 'Another dog will wee everywhere and turn my lawn into even more of a spotty mess. And there'll be no cats. They only come to you when they feel like it; not when you call them. I hate cats. They're up themselves.'

Two hands up, now thumbs together and pointers out. What-*everrrr*.

'Khhhhhheeeeaah!'

It was a cat kind of noise. Definitely. Dad was such a dog. He'd been kidding the whole time. What a cool present. Like, totally flip. (I made that up. Now I'm trying to get other kids at school to say 'flip', too. It'd be cool to be the one to invent something that everyone else copied.) 'I'm coming, Kitty,' I said. 'Everything's going to be flip, Kitty. Or cool, if you're not old enough to know flip.'

'Khhhhhheeeeaah!' Then *rattle rattle*. My new cat sounded happy to see me.

I put Tedalina on the floor and stepped onto one of the beams. Dad had shown me how to do it, when he was putting the floor in. He said it was a bit of a pain and that was why I was so surprised he'd hidden my Christmas kitty all the way back there in the roof-space. I knew for sure that Mum hated coming up here, which meant Dad would be the one who was up and down every day and night, feeding my little pooddy cat.

How come Mum was so paranoid?

'Nearly there, Kitty.' Kitty didn't make any noise, or rattle this time. She was so excited to see me she couldn't move.

I stuck close to the chimney, reached out and used it for balance.

Closer. Closer. I kept the torch light on the roof beams in front of me. Nearly there. Then I went down on my hands and knees. I wanted to be on the kitten's level when I saw it, so it wouldn't be scared of big old me. Steve Irwin told me that in a wildlife documentary on TV. It makes animals feel less threatened. I think. Or did it threaten them? No. Steve was always crawling around; this was the right thing to do.

I was almost past the chimney and still couldn't see anything. Dad had gone completely overboard this time. I put the torch in my mouth and crawled. Still no noise from my kitty. She had to be even more excited than me.

Finally. Past the chimney. There was nothing else for my cat to hide behind. So, still with the torch in my mouth, I moved the spotlight from the beam I was crawling on.

And onto a cage.

Then 'REEEOOOOOOOW!' It was more of a smack than a rattle, as a giant possum launched itself from the back end of the cage to the front. The noise was worse than the worst squeal you've ever heard from a beast in a horror movie. I think the thing wanted to kill me. I screamed, jumped up and back at the same time and started running before my feet even hit the ground.

I didn't even care if I was stepping on the beams or not. The torch was gone and then, in the middle of my squealing and the possum's screaming, my foot disappeared. It went straight through the fluffy insulation stuff.

And through the ceiling.

Ow. Owowowow!

My other foot disappeared as well, only on the other side of the roof beam.

The possum was still going psycho. I'd dropped the torch right in front of the cage, and the light was shining right into its face. It was huge; as big as a rottweiler.

I was stuck.

I couldn't pull either of my feet out from the ceiling, because the metal was nearly killing me. Then screaming started to hurt, so I stopped doing that, too.

There was light coming from the pull-down ladder, which was good, but it shone on the possum, too, which was bad. Every time I looked at it, the thing was staring at me, so I tried not to look.

I tried to drag my feet back up again, but it was no good. It killed!

I was in so much trouble, which was like so not fair. None of this was my fault. If Mum and Dad had done what they always did and hidden my presents in a normal place, I wouldn't have been forced to get up in the roof anyway. And if I wasn't in the roof I wouldn't have been scared by the possum and stepped off the beams and gone through the ceiling.

But I already knew they wouldn't see it that way. They never did.

Then there was a new noise. A car. Mum was home. I tried to pull my legs back again, but it was hopeless.

There was no noise when the door opened, but a definite bang when it shut.

'Mandy, we're home.' It was Dad!

Disaster.

And Mum. 'Hon-ey,' she sang. Double disaster. I was going to get in twice as much trouble with the two of them together.

'Mandy? Are you home? We've got a big surprise!'

'Yeah,' I yelled. 'So have I.'

'What is it?' Dad yelled down the hallway. I could

hear their feet thumping closer.

'I'll tell you, but you're not allowed to look up.'

Their footsteps stopped.

That was when Mum started screaming.

Incy Wincy Spider

Incy Wincy Spider saw Rudolph on the roof.
He really loved that reindeer and jumped up on his hoof.
But Rudolph hated spiders – can you guess what happened next?
He trampled poor old Incy Wince and snapped all his eight legs.
Ouch!

CAMP BOW WOW

'Oh, Fido, Great God of Dog. Please, I beg you. I promise I'll be good. I will.' I tried not to pant while I was praying to the great one, but the long-legs packing their suitcases had me in a lather. We don't pant just when we're toasty; it can be a nerves or an excitement thing, too.

That first sight of them packing got me really hot under the collar. What was left of my tail was spinning, I had slobber on the drip and I reckoned if I didn't start a hole soon I'd burst.

But then they looked at me as if I had a date with the vet. That turned me round faster than whenever Dopey and I chose different sides of a telegraph pole. I hate walking on the lead. I'm a forty-year-old, so I'm quite capable of crossing a road by myself. I'm not some young pup.

After they gave me the you're-going-to-the-vet-for-needles look, the little long-legs with the big hands said something like, 'It'll be all right, Spanner. You'll see.' But he said it in a baby voice, while he rubbed that twitchy bit where the hair used to grow, just above my tail. 'Iddill bee aw-wight, Spanner. You'll see, yes you will. Yes-you-will-you'll-see-you-will. Oh, you like that, don't you! You're a good widdle boy. Yes-you-are-you-are-you-are!'

But I didn't like it. I loved it – right up until he stopped.

I'd lost all feeling in my legs and was halfway to the floor, all ready to roll over and show him my gut so he could give that a scratch as well.

'Too many things to do, Spanner. Sorry, mate!' From the way he said it, I didn't think lying on the couch watching TV would be a big priority, but apparently he did. I tried to jump up there with him, but got pushed back to earth almost before I'd left it. Then I backed up on the foot he'd left on the ground – hoping to have a bit of a grind – but I only managed a boot up the bum for my trouble.

The older long-legs hardly bothered with me. I tried getting under their feet to find out what was going on, but only managed another couple of boots in the bum. That was when I started sulking.

It always gets 'em. I arch my back, make my legs go all stiff and walk on my toes. I've got no idea what I look like, but it scares the long-legs bigtime – almost as much as when I cower as if I'm going to get clubbed. They hate that.

So I turned the sad dog eyes on the leader. That's pretty hard for me to do, because I don't have big eyes. Cocker spaniels and bassets are brilliant at the sad dog eyes. They hang their ears forward by dropping their heads and suddenly they're the glummest dogs in the world.

But I did my best and eventually one of them noticed. It was the one who grunted more than he talked. We got along the best. 'Somefin's wrong wif the dog. What's up, Span?'

I made a little noise. *Rrrrrrr.*

'What's that, bro? Not feeling well?'

Rrrrr, rorrrrrr.

'He's not good, Mum.' My favourite long-leg was right about that. I needed to know what was going on. I'm no idiot. I'm not a cat. If the long-legs were going somewhere, either I was going with them, or I wasn't.

Things were going to be good, or bad. Simple as that.

While I waited for the queen of the long-legs to check on me, I prayed to Fido, the Great God of Dog for good. I wanted good.

I deserved it.

The queen of the long-legs stopped throwing clothes on the floor. (It's all right when *she* does it, but if *I* take the clothes off the line, I get hammered.) She got down on her knees and grabbed my face in both her hands. She shook it, in a friendly-hurty way.

'Oh, please great and generous Fido. Please, please please.' I gave her my saddest sad eyes ever. By the way she was looking at me I knew the answer was going to be as bad as it could be. 'If you give me what I want, I'll stop peeing on the lawn. I'll stop eating your shoes. I won't bark at night. I won't run away or sneak little poohs in the house or vomit in the car. Promise I won't. Just make the news good.'

She kissed me on top of the head and I knew right then that she was going to betray me. She'd say, 'Oh, Spanner honey, it's not up to me. Sorry, pup. But we're going to have to take you with us.'

I cocked my head to one side. Oh, come on, just get on with it!

'Sorry, Spanner,' she started, 'but – '

I'd have to run away. There was nothing else for it. The butcher liked me. He'd give me food. Bin night was better than ever, now that everyone had to recycle. Food was usually in the middle bin. (If only someone would invent colour, they could colour-code the bins and it'd be even easier.)

'Spanner. Don't look so sad. It won't be for long.'

Rrrr, Roorrrrr. Rirr! 'Fido, you dog, how could you do this to me?' I was going with them. I'd be stuffed into the back of the car, squashed up somewhere between the luggage and the picnic basket, which was always locked. Well, fine. I'd get the old bone I buried and bring it with me. I'd vomit everywhere and dribble on EVERYTHING. This was the last time I'd leave Fido a sacrifice of real meat!

The queen of the long-legs interrupted my thinking. 'And we'll be back before you know it.'

Hang on a second.

'You don't mind, do you? We'll miss you.' And then she said it – the one word I wanted to hear. But she said it as if it was bad. 'It'll be like a holiday,' she said. 'You like the kennel, don't you?'

That was the word: 'kennel'. Out it came slowly. 'K-E-N-N-E-L'!

Thank you, Great and Powerful One. Forgive me for ever having doubted you! The long-legs weren't the only ones going on holiday; I was, too. I was going to Camp Bow Wow.

Yes, yes, yes! All those other dogs, the fast food, breakfast, afternoon tea. The exercise yard. The different smells. And – and maybe *she'd* be there, too! I felt my legs go weak as if someone was rubbing my bald spot again. I had to sit down. Then I rolled over and tried to get my gut off the ground and close to the queen's tickling fingers.

Oh, that was good! A tummy tickle and a holiday at Camp Bow Wow. The queen of the long-legs got up and went on packing.

I hit the backyard and started to dig. It was time to celebrate and I had just the bone for it.

Sometimes I put my head out the window and let my tongue flap against my cheek. Sometimes I slobber. Sometimes I scratch the underside of my tail by grinding it on the hand brake. Cars are great if you're not stuck in the back. There's so much to do!

'We're here,' the king of the long-legs said. 'Be a good boy, eh?'

I started bouncing around the car even before we'd stopped. I'm one of very few dogs who can do a full three-sixty-degree leap to the left and the right. It took ages to learn how to do it and this was where I learnt it – at Camp Bow Wow. Rastus taught me. He's the labradoodle with dreads. A cool pup, but totally psycho, he was in the pen next to me last year, but had to leave early. He's got one great joke and he tells it all the time. How many dogs does it take to change a light bulb? None – we can see in the dark. Pretty funny, right? It was going to be great to see him again.

The king of the long-legs opened his door and I bolted.

Ah, the smells. On the gate post there must have been a million different wees. Paradise! But there was only one I was looking for. *Sniff sniff.* 'Where are ya? Come on, I know you're here somewhere.' *Sniff sniff.*

The king pulled me up by the lead before I got to the shrubs. 'Come on, Spanner. Plenty of time for that.' I let a quick dribble go in the middle of no-man's-land and I tried to be cool while he checked me in.

Rrrrr, rirr! 'Hurry up – I can't stand it. I've got to get in there!'

Finally the king squatted in front of me and rubbed my ears. 'Be a good boy, Span. It won't be long and we'll be back before you know it.'

Rrrrrr. 'Yeah, bye.' I gave him a quick lick, but didn't look back as the kennel guy took me by the lead, up the path and into Camp Bow Wow. Dogs were barking already. The place was going off.

'G'day, Spanner!'

'How are you, mate?'

'You've put on weight, ya monster. What are ya – part labrador?'

'Look who's talking!' I laughed. It was great to be back. There were a million more smells and I dribbled a bit on every kennel door I walked past, just to say hi. It was a mark of respect. I was so happy.

Then I saw her. She was even more beautiful than last year. Had it been that long?

She was up the end, asleep – or just pretending– her fluffy white coat like a blanket of clouds around her face. She'd let it grow. I stuck my tail straight up in the air and dropped my head, just a bit. 'Aroof!' It didn't come out as cool as I'd wanted it to. Even so, she opened her eyes and looked at me as if I was the only dog in the kennel. I wanted to rush to her, lick her face, smell her bottom, have her bury her nose in mine. But why rush? There'd be time for that. Plenty of it. We'd get yard duty together again for sure.

She lifted that gorgeous head off her mat, parted her thin black lips and gave me a look at her teeth. 'Hirrrrrr. Hello, Spanner.' It was almost a purr.

'G'day, Belle. You look great. I've missed –'

'A-ROO. A-ROO-ROO-ROOH!'

What the –?

A huge black rottweiler with a head the size of a small car smashed into the wire I was wizzing on. It scared the love and more right out of me! I jumped to the other side of the aisle and cowered there like a pup. First rule of dog fighting: get down, stay low, assume a position of weakness, while you assess the situation. But always, always, be ready to rock and roll.

I'd never seen him before.

'Don't even think about it, you liddle weasel!' He even had a rottweiler accent. It was as if he didn't breathe between words, like that guy in the action movies. 'Zat iss my Belle now – not yours. Unnerstand? Tell him, puzzy cat!'

I looked at Belle, but she turned away. All the dogs did. The yapping stopped and they slunk back to their mats.

'A-ROO. A-ROO-ROO-ROOH! My name iss Brutus Maximus. Zis iss my kennel now. And Belle iss my baybee. A-ROOOOOOH!'

The handler gave his cage a quick boot. 'Settle down, Brutus!' But this only sent the big dog into a frenzy.

'A-ROOROOROO! I rip your big ztoobid head off your ztoobid weak liddle shoulders. You are a kitten and I am Brutus Maximus. I eat you and pooh you out my bottom!'

'Tough when you're protected by the cage, aren't you, Brutus!' said the handler.

'Zen open ze cage!' bellowed the big dog.

The long-leg pulled me away. I'd been dying to get to my pen and have a sniff around, but the vibe was gone. Brutus Maximus had barked it away.

'Good on ya, Spanner,' said the handler. 'Nice to

102

have you back.'

I gave my tail a bit of a wag.

'Whaart are you so happy about, loozer?' bleated Brutus.

'Yeah, yeah!' I said. I was tough in my cage, too. He was across the isle, four cages down.

Belle was still up the end. I could see her, but so could Brutus. I gave her a look that said, "What's going on?"

'I zaid, don't even think about it.' What a mongrel. I wondered if he ever slept.

'You can't tell me where I can look, Brutus.' I sat down to hide the shaking in my back legs.

'No? Okay, fine, tough-puppy.' He sounded almost chirpy, but then the growl started. 'Look at her ass much ass you like and next time I get near you I eat you and pooh you.'

Belle crossed her legs and laid her head on her paws. She looked from me to Brutus and back to me again. I couldn't work out the look she was giving me; it was kind of sad and happy. Happy to see me, or sad to have Brutus at Camp Bow Wow? Or sad to see me and happy to see Brutus? Or sad that I had interrupted her and Brutus being so happy? Or happy that I would save her from her sad life with Brutus?

Or maybe she wasn't thinking anything. But what if she was? Was it worse if she wasn't?

What about Brutus? I watched him trying to eat his food bowl. What a thug! He had his bum pressed up against the wire, with that stump of a tail pushing through. It was wagging as if it had a life of its own. So did he love Belle, or just like her? I couldn't see them sharing a kennel together – not the way she would with me. I'd let her nuzzle up next to me, put her head on my neck, or anywhere else she wanted. We'd lie around like puppies, all over each other. But Brutus would squash her. Then he'd probably eat her. And pooh her. Was he really that tough? Did he have a weak spot? Was he scared of anything or anyone?

Sometimes I hate being a dog – especially a dog without answers.

My salvation was in the exercise yard that after-noon. Guido, the bum-reader, was working the fence, getting the dirt on whoever was at Camp Bow Wow at the time. All dogs leave a trail and Guido is the master at finding them.

I didn't want to interrupt him straightaway, so I went to the fence and looked out over the valley below. If this wasn't the perfect spot for a holiday, what was?

'G'day, Spanner,' said Guido. He was beside me now.

'Guido, great to see you.' We sniffed each other's bums as a sign of respect. Mmmmm. What had he eaten to smell like that? 'I've got a problem, pal,' I said.

'I know,' he snorted. 'It's written all over your bum. I could tell when I trotted up.' Guido really is a top reader – probably the most famous one in the world.

A bum-reader's like a fortune-teller, only he doesn't work on your paw or your eyeball. 'Listen, pup. Your left cheek's all wobbly, you're puckered on the right side and your stump looks as if it's run out of batteries.'

'That bad, huh?'

'Worse.' He went behind me and stared. 'The way the hair's matted together over there near your goolies tells me you're deeply depressed and – oh, hang on a minute. Look at this.'

'What? What is it?' I tried to get a look at my own bum, which was pretty stupid, I admit. I used to chase my own tail when I was a puppy, but after about a year I realised that if I didn't quit I'd go nuts. Besides, they cut my tail my off and that took most of the fun out of it.

'You're in love and you can't get her, can you? There's something in your way. I see a problem. A big black problem. You're away from it now, but it'll come closer. It haunts you. Taunts you. Let me see.' There was a quick sniff. Then he backed off a bit. 'Is it Bogan Monstrous? Bogus? Brutus? Is it Brutus Mastermass?'

'Brutus Maximus! That's what he calls himself. Jeez. You can tell all that from looking at my bum?'

'Don't be a wag! I was having a chat to Belle. She told me everything.'

'Well, what am I going to do, Guido? He's massive.

He reckons he'll rip me to bits if I go near her. He's insane, too. He's eaten two food bowls already and they're made of metal. Now they just squish his food through the wire mesh. But, worst of all, I think Belle likes him.'

'You're right.' He lowered his head when he said it.

'She does like him? Oh, God of Dog. I only said that so you'd say she didn't.'

'Careful, Spanner. If your bum droops any closer to the ground, it'll fall off. I meant you were right about Brutus being psycho; not about Belle liking him. Besides, she said she had a sniff with a rottweiler once before and it wasn't what she'd thought it was going to be.'

'There's been other dogs besides me?'

'Oh, grow up, Spanner! I'll have a look at him when I get a chance. It won't take long. Every dog's got a weakness and when I find his, we'll work out a plan. You'll get your girlie, pup, I promise. It's written all over your bum. Your future's behind you, believe me.'

We sniffed each other goodbye. He went back to finding smells along the fence, while I laid a trail near the gate so if Belle came in she'd know I'd been round and that I loved her.

But as I was leaving the exercise yard, Brutus was on his way in. He growled and I shied away. 'A-ROO

ROO ROO,' he roared at me after smelling the ground. 'Been leaving luff letters, have you, Romeo? Well, I luff you, too! I luff you zo much I would like to chomp you up into liddle bite-sized piezes, eat you and pooh you! A-ROO ROO ROO!'

Mongrel!

The long-leg let me stop by Belle's pen on the way back to my own. She put her perfect little nose through the wire and I sniffed and licked and kissed and felt as if Camp Bow Wow was back to normal. She said she didn't love Brutus; in fact she hated him. It was me she loved.

The long-leg didn't give us nearly enough time together to talk about the big private things, but from my pen I could see her and we talked about all the other stuff. Other dogs joined in. There were jokes and stories. Crusty broke a leg chasing a car. Flop speared himself with a stick he was chasing. Benny caught fire when he was asleep. Angie had to go to the hospital after eating leftover green curry that the idiot long-legs didn't check for chillies. One of the labradors had got so fat she couldn't clean herself properly. Ugh!

Then we had a farting contest. Everyone tried to do three-sixties from a standing start. It was all good – exactly the way Camp Bow Wow had always been.

And then Brutus came back. 'A-ROO ROO ROO.' Suddenly all the stories were about him. 'I like to chaze rabbits and when I catch zem I eat zem and pooh zem. I caught a possum once. I eat it. Haz anyone ever eaten and poohed a cat? I have! They got sharp teeth. ROO ROO.'

Everyone else stopped yapping. There wasn't much to say. I turned around so I couldn't see him and muttered, 'Go and chase your tail, you big dufus.'

'I ate it already. Just like I'm going to do to you. Now shuddup while I get some zleep. Everybody!' He circled three times, dropped and let his meaty head fall on top of his paws. Within seconds he was snoring.

'I hope he bites his tongue,' said Benny.

'He'd probably eat it. And zen he would pooh it!' We all laughed, but quietly so the big lump didn't wake up. While he slept, Camp Bow Wow got back to normal, at half the volume. What a top spot for a break!

Guido came back from the yard and stopped by my pen. 'Good news,' he muttered.

'Yeah? His owner ties him to the back of his ute, forgets he's there and drives to Queensland?'

'Maybe,' said Guido. 'I got a good look at him in the yard. You're right. He's massive, isn't he? And he's got a very busy bum. It's twitching all the time – that's not a good sign. He's got a very tight left side, but once it gets to the action he's a bit loose. He's scared of spiders and thunder. If we could get a storm organised, he'd be petrified. Maybe we should sing "Incy Wincy Spider" over and over to get inside his head, I dunno.'

'Is that all you've got?' I was desperate. The big dog wasn't ruining just my holiday; he was wrecking everyone's.

'Mmmm, there was something else.' Guido was whispering to me, but staring at the bum of the dog in the pen next to me. 'You need to eat more bran, fella.'

'Guido! What about Brutus?'

'Ah, yeah. But seriously, that dog next to you has a sagging bum like a dog of ninety, and he's only twentysomething –'

'Oh, for Fido's sake!'

'Yeah, sorry.' He was back. 'Brutus is going on a trip, and I don't think he'll like it. He's in for a rough time. Really rough. Be patient, because I don't think he's going to be a problem for you anymore – not after this arvo. He's been a bad boy and it's time to pay up. He's going away for a long, long time.'

'You don't mean – '

'Yep!'

'You can tell they're going to put him down from the marks and lines and shape of his bum?'

'Nope, I didn't read it. I heard the long-legs talking about it.'

The dogs nearest to us had been listening. Then suddenly everyone was. The whole place had gone quiet. No one liked to hear that a dog was being put to sleep, even if they did deserve it.

'How does he go?' asked Belle. 'Needle? Green dream?'

'They're going to stud him,' barked Guido. 'He's off to some place called a stud farm. They said he's a stud dog. I don't even know what that is, but it sounds like a shocking way to go. Like some sort of firing squad.'

'Poor guy,' I said. 'No wonder he's so angry. He's a stud dog.'

'And he's going this afternoon, but he doesn't know yet.'

'Who doesn't know what?' grumped the big black dog. He lifted his head off his mat to drink some water.

'Nothing,' said most of the dogs. 'No one here knows a thing.'

'Tell me zomething I don't know.' Brutus was on his feet now. He drank more water, then started to eat the water bowl. No one said much as he worked his way through it. I suppose we were all thinking the same thing. How bad would a dog have to be to get sent to a stud farm? I knew there were good reasons to be scared of him – he was obviously a monster – but, still –

A long-leg came in just as he was finishing off the bowl. They'd have to find tougher metal for dogs like him. 'Righto, Brutus. Holiday's over, let's go.' Brutus growled, but let the long-leg slip the collar over his head.

'Don't even think about talking to my girlie!' He snarled at me.

'Yeah, righto, Brutus. But I don't know what you think you're going to do about it.' I was in my pen. I was safe.

'A-ROO ROO ROO!' He launched himself at the wire between us. 'I am Brutus Maximus. Zere is nothing I cannot do. I will eat you up, you ztoobid liddle dog! And then – '

'Yeah yeah! You'll pooh me,' I said.

'Zat is right.' He took a step back and looked at me with his head to one side. 'How did you know?'

'You're such a loser, Brutus. You talk tough, you act tough, but you're really just a big bully and no one likes bullies. You couldn't leave it alone, could you? Loser!' All the other dogs cheered and barked. The place went off. Now that Brutus was leaving, Camp Bow Wow was having a very good day!

Brutus looked around at all the dogs laughing and cheering. His hackles went up, he swelled to twice his size. He pulled against his lead as he tried to get away from the long-leg and nearer to one of us. 'I'll get you and I'll eat you. Each and every one. You'll be zorry!'

'Come on, Brutus,' laughed the long-leg. 'It's the stud farm for you.'

'Sucked in, Bogan Maximum! You're going to the stud farm.' Brutus had put paid to any pity we'd had for him.

'Everyone say goodbye,' said the long-leg, and we did.

But Brutus just kept yelling. 'I am Brutus Maximus and on my return I will unleash hell!'

The long-leg dragged him, scratching and barking the whole way. We all cheered again. Then, when the long-leg finally got him to the door, he said, 'Come on, big fella. It's okay. You'll be back before you know it.'

'Back?' I looked at Guido. He gulped. 'Didn't they say how long he goes to this stud farm for?' I said.

'Just this afternoon,' said Guido. He was trying to hide behind his fringe. 'I did a second reading and I think he comes back tonight. You know what a stud farm is for, don't you? If it works, there'll be more Brutuses on the way. Did I forget to tell you?'

That shut the lot of us up.

I looked along the aisle at all the wire mesh between me and Belle.

And suddenly being on holiday with the king and queen of the long-legs was looking good.

TIPS FOR DEALING WITH THE RELATIVES

Talking to the rellies on Christmas Day is a lot like talking to them on your birthday – only they want to talk about their own presents as much as you want to talk about yours.

So first, if you're going to answer the phone, you should say, 'Merry Christmas'.

Do not answer phone with, 'Yeah?'

Or 'Whadyawant?'

Or 'Whoisit?'

Definitely do not say, 'Mum's on the toilet.'

Or 'Dad's on the toilet, too. I think he's growing a tail. A smelly one!'

You just say, 'Merry Christmas' brightly, because the person on the other end might have a present for you. That present might be money, and if you're rude they could steam the envelope open, halve the cash and close it again.

It happens, believe me.

You see, it might be a long lost auntie about to die with money to give away – you never know, although you might think that stuff only happens in movies. Ideas for movies do come from somewhere. So, if it's going to happen, it might as well happen to you.

Secondly, it's really not a bad idea to have the big answers ready.

When Uncle Barry rings up and says, 'What'd you think of those fish-hooks I sent you?' It'd be better not to say, 'Gee, Uncle Barry, they suck. And they're rusty. Did you think about not using them before giving them away as a present, or did you think you should test them to make sure they worked? They're fish-hooks, you goombah. It's not as if they need batteries.'

Even rusty fish-hooks are better than none.

Actually, that is a total lie. Rusty fish-hooks aren't good for anything – except providing your parents with a reason to give you a tetanus shot after you jag one in your finger.

You might have to practise the answer to the general do-you-like-what-I-gave-you question. You ready?

Practise. 'I LOVE it!'

Not, 'I like it.'

Not, 'Yeah, s'all right.'

'I LOVE it!' This might just inspire Uncle Barry to try harder next year. And it might not. He might be so happy you liked his skanky hooks that next year he'll give you a couple of sinkers too. He might be that rich rello we were talking about before.

Maybe you should write a list of what you got for Christmas and keep it in your front pocket, where you can find it. Recite the list, but with feeling.

And don't go on with, 'Christmas is an important time for everyone', even if you think it is. The rellies will know you're trying to be smart – and that's not good groundwork for your next birthday present, or certainly your next Christmas gift!

Always finish off by saying thanks. If it's a grand-parent say, 'Thank you *very* much.' And if it's some-one really boring, say, 'Thanks, I'll put my sister on', even if she's already spoken to them. Sisters hate that.

32 ~~AUGUST~~ 1 SEPT

~~32 August~~ 1 Sept

Dear Santa,

How's it hangin?

This year I've decided it's time to grow up. I like being a kid and getting presents and everything, but there are people in this world who need presents from you more than I do. Crazy, isn't it? But there are.

You know who I'm talking about, don't you! That's right — my sister, Emma. I was thinking that instead of giving something to me, you could give her something. So my present to her would really be your present to me that you give to her.

Cool, huh?

I'll even tell you what it should be, so you don't have to think about it or anything. It'll be a no-brainer, yeah?

Okay, my sister Emma is thirteen.

She wears a training bra, but she doesn't need to. It's stuffed with tissues — but don't give her boobs. That'd suck. She'd love boobs. Yesterday she shaved her legs for the first time and now they're bright red, because she didn't use shaving cream. She'd probably love shaving cream.

She thinks she's a pop star, but she can't sing. She's in love with Johnny Blueberry from that band — but please please please don't give her concert tickets like she wants for when they come out in February.

I want you to give her something special. Something she'll never forget!

Santa, I want you to give my sister a zit. What do you reckon? Can you do that for me? Just one — not stacks of them. I don't want her playing join-the-dots on her face, or anything like that. Just one pimple. It's what she wants. I'm not being mean, I promise.

See, I read it in her diary. She keeps it hidden in her top drawer. She doesn't think I'll look there, because she thinks I hate touching her undies.

In her diary it says, "Dear Diary, I love Johnny Blueberry, but I don't think he'll like my pimple. So when Blueberry come to Oz, I'd like to have no zits at all. Wouldn't it be cool if I never had another zit after I get rid of this Mount Vesuvius that's weighing down my head?"

And her diary wrote back, "That would be cool".

Then she wrote, "Maybe I could have all my zits for the rest of my life right now — in one zit. That'd be even cooler."

"That would be the coolest," her diary wrote back.

And then my sister wrote a whole bunch of other stuff about Johnny Blueberry. It was off. She wrote how she wanted him to sing a song that was just for her, and how she wanted him to pull her out of the crowd at the concert and dance with her like he does with that girl in the Blueberry video. And she could kiss him, maybe. I'm telling you, Santa, this stuff was totally off. And dumb. They're things you don't need to know about.

Believe me, I'm doing you a favour by not telling you more.

Anyway. Do you give kids zits? It'd be totally mad if she could have what she wants.

How about one big angry boil? A giant red volcano, oozing pus instead of lava.

Doh! Got to go. She's busted me writing to you. She reckons it's childish.

Yeah, right. I'll write again soon,

Brian Hadrill

PS. Maybe I could have a surfboard, too?

And thanks for the snow boots last year. Next time, can you talk to the weather-man to make sure it's going to snow?

12 September
(About two weeks before my team would've won the
Grand Final if they'd made the finals in the first
place, and six months before Blueberry play the
Entertainment Centre.)

Dear Father Christmas
(I know I used to call you Santa, but that seems a
bit childish, now that I'm a teenager).

Like, how are things?

Rad.

I've been so thinking about this since last
Christmas (when you were still Santa) and I was
wondering if I could ask you a favour. I've got this
brother. His name's Brian. Can you make him
disappear?

Just kidding. But that'd be cool, wouldn't it?
The coolest? You're funny, Santa – I mean, Father
Christmas. But you're not a magician, so. Um.
Like.

My brother Brian wants a surfboard.

Do you think you could give him one? He needs an interest – something other than being annoying – which he's like the world champion at. Coz if he had a surfboard, that'd be more interesting than bugging me. Right?

Cool.

Emma Hadrill

13 September

Dear Santa-dude,

Hi, it's me again, Brian Hadrill.
Remember me?

Have you been working up a big pot of pus for my
sister? I've been thinking about the zit you're going
to give her. At least, I've been thinking about where
you might put it.

There's no point putting it on her back,
because no one'll see it there — unless it's
massive. Is it massive? If it is, she'd be
like the Hunchback of Ellesten Court.
That'd be pretty funny, actually. But if
it's not massive, if it's big but not

Massive pimple ↓

ginormous, then she'll just hide it. She'll wear a big
jumper or something.

I think her face would be the acest spot to put it.
On her nose would be even acer. Right on the end
of it. We could call her Rudolph. You like carols,
don't you?

We could sing one to her. Instead of 'Rudolph the Red Nosed Reindeer' we could sing this.

Emma, my pus-nosed sister,

Has a red and pusy nose.

And if you ever saw it,

You would see the way it blows.

That's not a zit,

this is a zit!!

Oh, wait. Doh! Such a suck! If you put it on her nose, she'd be able to cover it with make up, and when the pus dribbled out of it, she could pretend it was snot. She'd just say she had a cold. She's a pretty good actor, my sister. She might be able to get away with it.

Spew.

Our secret, remember.

Got to go!

Brian Hadrill

PS How about a Brad Bowman skateboard? I saw one on ebay. I've got no idea who Brad Bowman is (the photo was totally old), but the board was really expensive, so he must be cool. Thanks. You don't have to, of course. Because I don't really want anything for me.

See ya, wouldn't wanna be ya. (Yes I would!)

Brian

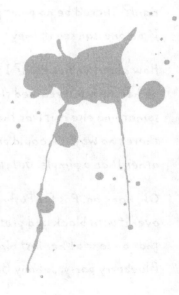

29 September

Hey, Santa,

My footy team bite. I should've aksed you for a
Grand Final, hey? Hadders again. (Brian Hadrill. I just
picked up Hadders as a nickname. Do you like it?)

Where are you up to with my sister's zit? Have you
figured out where you're going to put it? Not on her
back, right? Or her arm or behind her knee or
anywhere like that, okay. It's got to be on her face,
right? There'd be no point putting it anywhere else.
If no one can see it, they won't know it's there.

How about on her chin? I thought you could put it
on her nose, but realised she could pretend it was
something else if it was there. If it was on her chin,
there's no way she could pretend it was anything
other than a pimple. Got it?

Oh, hang on. P is for Pusbrain! She might colour
over it with black and pretend it's a goatee. She did
that once — at her last birthday party. It was a
Blueberry party. Johnny Blueberry's got a goatee,

so my sister drew one on her chin with texta and everyone said it was the coolest thing ever. By the end of the party she said all the girls had drawn one on too.

Dumb!

If her Christmas zit's anything like as big as I hope it's going to be, Emma'll do anything to cover it.

Once, in her diary, she wrote, "Dear Diary, I wish I had a goatee like Johnny Blueberry. Wouldn't that be cool?"

And her diary wrote back, "That would be the coolest". Her diary always agrees with her. It's as dumb as she is.

Doh! Better split, Santa. The Simpsons are on. I'll write again soon.

Thanks,

Brian Hadrill

PS I was thinking that my bike's a bit small for me. Maybe I could get another one. Maybe.

29 MOvember

Dear Father Christmas,

My brother has tried to grow a MOustache for MOvember because my dad did. Unfortunately, my brother is eleven. He stands in front of the mirror, licks his fingers and tries to curl his peach fuzz into a mo.

L is for Loser, right?

He's all right, though, I suppose.
For a LOSER!

Just wondering if you managed to get any tickets to the Blueberry concert next year. I missed out. Maybe I can like get some on ebay. I hope so. It'd be cooler if I could get some from you for Christmas, though. Dude, dude, dude!

I love Blueberry. I've only told my diary this, but you're cool. I know you won't tell anyone. Sometimes I wish I had a goatee like Johnny Blueberry. Sometimes I wish I was Johnny Blueberry – just so I could know what it's like to be near him. Is that like psycho, or what? But if I was him, I'd know what he was thinking and the kind of girls he liked and I could dress like one of them and he'd like pull me out of the crowd at the concert and dance with me, just like he does with that girl in the video.

Oh, I'd love to be THAT girl.

Hey, Santa. Brian's being a pain, but kind of nice, too. Boys are WEIRD.

I got him something for Christmas, so I thought I'd tell you. That way you won't like double up. It's a skateboard. I made it in woodwork. He'll love it.

Maybe you should get him some new skateboard wheels. And maybe some trucks, too. They're the silver bits that hold the wheels to the deck.

Choice, Santa. Good one, Bhagwan!

Love,

Emma Hadrill

13 December

Santaaaaaaah, dude, it's a Friday, and it's the 13th. Creepy.

Yo, bro, got rid of the mo! But how cool was MOvember? Hadders, again. I reckon this'll be the last time I write before Christmas. Things are heating up — not just the weather — but school's on the way out, hols are on the way in. Jessica Winter's staring at me all the time, when I'm not looking at her. But whenever I do look, she turns away. Wicked!

Hey, Santa, we need to decide on a place for my sister's zit. I think I've got it.

I reckon it should be between her eyes. Right in the middle, and maybe up a bit. Like the Cyclops's third eye — too high to be hidden by sunglasses and too low for her fringe. Did you know she cut it last week? Oh, man. She did it to copy that bonehead, Johnny Blueberry. He's chopped all his hair off at the front, but left it long at the back and sides. What a — I don't know what he is!

So, are we cool, Santa?

I want absolutely nothing for Christmas (from you) except a big zit for my sister. And can you stick it in the middle of her forehead?

Cool.

We rock! You and me, right?

Your mate,

Hadders

PS If you really really really wanted to bring me something, what about a remote control surfer? I don't even know if you can get them, but I so want one.

24 December

Dear Father Christmas,

I have no idea what my brother's up to. He keeps looking at my face as if he's waiting for something to happen. Like maybe like something is going to pop up spontaneously and he wants to be there when it happens. He's WIGGING me out!

I feel as if something really big is about to happen, but I can't work out what.

You've got the tickets, haven't you?

Cool.

You rule, Father Christmas.

Love,

Emma

26 December

Dear Santa,

You legend!

Brian Hadders Hadrill

26 December

Dear Father Christmas,

How did you know? Blueberry tickets and zit cream.

You're the best!

Love,

Emma

MORE JOKES

Patient: Doctor, what does the
X-ray of my head show?
Doctor: Absolutely nothing!

What's Christmas called in England?
Yule Britannia!

Why are Christmas trees like bad knitters?
They both drop their needles!

What do monkeys sing at Christmas?
Jungle Bells, Jungle Bells!

What did the bald man say when he
got a comb for Christmas?
Thanks, I'll never part with it!

Why is a burning candle like being thirsty?
Beacause a little water ends both of them!

What do you get if you cross an apple
with a Christmas tree?
A pineapple!

What do you give a train driver for Christmas?
Platform shoes!

What did the big candle say to the little candle?
I'm going out tonight!

What happens to you at Christmas?
Yule be happy!

How long does it take to burn a candle down?
About a wick!

What did Adam say on the day
before Christmas?
It's Christmas, Eve!

How do you make an idiot laugh on Boxing Day?
Tell him a joke on Christmas Eve!

What do you have in December that you don't have
in any other month?
The letter "D"!

What does Father Christmas suffer
from if he gets stuck in a chimney?
Santa Claustrophobia!

What do you call a letter sent up the chimney on
Christmas Eve?
Blackmail!

Who delivers the cat's Christmas presents?
Santa Paws!

Why is Santa like a bear on Christmas Eve?
Because he's Sooty!

Who delivers elephants' Christmas presents?
Elephanta Claus!

How many chimneys does Father Christmas go down?
Stacks!

Why does Father Christmas go down the chimney?
Because it soots him!

T·WAS· THE· NiGHT

Twas the night before Christmas,
when all through the house
not a thing was stirring –
not even the mouse.

The stockings were hung by the front door with care
to trick old St Nick – he'd come if he dared.
Me and Thommo weren't nestled all snug in our beds.
We were hiding out back. There was fun in our heads.

Mum'd gone on the couch, the dog in her lap
and Dad on the can for a pre-Christmas crap,
when out in the dust there arose such a clatter.
It had to be Santa – he'd got even fatter.

It was good luck for him that there wasn't a chimney.
We lived underground – heard of Coober Pedy? –
where miners worked hard for most of the day,
though very few turned their sweat into pay.

(But that's not saying we don't like a laugh,
and when Santa turns up we don't do it by halves.)
We'd set him a trap that he couldn't see:
a tripwire, a hole and a bent-over tree.

We knew that he'd look for a place to get in,
so we wrote and told him, 'Turn right at the bin.'
And just like that he arrived on the night
with all of those reindeers – cripes, what a sight!

He hit our tripwire at a top little trot,
poor bloke, with that heavy sack that he'd got.
The wire flicked the tree, which uncovered the hole
and Santa went down like a big fat red mole.

He yelled as he fell and thumped when he landed.
It all went off perfectly, just as we'd planned it.
Then Santa said things that were naughty, not nice.
'We've got the wrong man,' I said. 'There'll be a price.'

'That sounds like your dad. And he's really aggro!
You've made a mistake, mate. You'll get it tomorrow.'
'We're all going to pay. He hates being tricked.'
Dad yelled something new and it sounded like 'flicks'.

But Thommo's attention was caught somewhere else.
'Are those bells the sound of the jolly red elf?'
Away in the distance a warm little glow
got gradually bigger; we heard, 'Ho, ho, ho.'

'To bed, mate, quick! If you're awake you get nothing.'
So we said good night. 'See ya! Hope you get something.'
Then I hit the pillow and went straight to sleep –
or pretended, at least. There wasn't a peep.

But it must have been real – didn't hear him come in.
I woke up to presents, some thick and some thin.
Then I heard Dad yelling from our hole out the back.
'Get me out of here, lad! I'll fix ya, ya brat!'

Incy Wincy Spider

Incy Wincy Spider had had about enough.
Santa Claus and Rudolph had played a little rough.
He thought he'd make a Christmas gift for his new worst old best friends,
but his head was squashed, his legs were snapped,
He'd wait for his revenge.
Ugh!

SUPA SANTA

Gary 'FJ' Peterson looked at himself in the bathroom mirror and smiled.

'Perfect. Ab-so-flippin-lutely perfect,' he thought out loud. The hat, the beard, the little bit of lipstick smudged over his cheeks to give them a warm, wintry glow. Of the seven Santas working Santa's Kingdom that December, he knew for a fact that he was the best. His 'Ho ho ho' was hot and his gut was real.

He cracked the bathroom door and had a look at the other Santas. *Bah!* What a joke. Fake beards, guts of stuffing, wigs – who did these blokes think they were kidding? They were only in it for the money. What a disgrace.

The kids who'd come to see Santa today deserved more than that. All kids did.

Even the kids who never got to see Santa were worth more than these pretenders were trying to be. One day these kids might meet other kids who'd never seen a supermarket Santa in their lives. They'd want to know what the experience was like, and any bozo could figure out that the report from the kid who'd seen one of these goons wouldn't be much good.

Gary had stood in line to see Santa when he was a five-year-old and the memory of it still made him shake.

His mum had taken him. Dad had been working, but Dad was always working back then. Mum had warned him, 'You'll work yourself to death!'

It was the one thing she'd been right about.

Gary and his mum'd got up early, caught the train all the way to town – "that's where the best Santas always are" – and they'd stood in line for about nine thousand hours. Santa was busy that day. Everyone wanted a piece of him, and from the look of his beard, a few had taken theirs, literally.

But when it was finally Gary FJ Peterson's turn on the big man's lap, he was a bit scared to take it. Santa's hat was crooked – just like his hair, which was stuck to his head in sweaty little curls. Gary could see Santa's pillow-gut pushing the buttons of his jacket apart. The

tag was sticking through the gap. Tontine. Santa's
boots were Blundstones.

Builders wore Blundstones. Carpenters and lab-
ourers and trendy TV gardeners trying to look normal
wore Blundstones. Not Santa. Blundstones were work
boots. Gary's dad wore Blundstones. In all the Christmas pictures, the real Santa wore shiny black boots –
sometimes with a silver buckle; sometimes not. That
might have depended on the heat or the cold or
maybe the fashion at the time the photo was taken.
Santa didn't sweat, he didn't stuff his suit with Tontine
pillows and he did not stink of rotten BO, garlic,
smokes or stale beer.

That's what this Santa smelt of. It was exactly the same smell as his dad's best mate, whose name was Angelo. He was Italian, but the old fashioned kind – not the hip kind of Australian Angelos you meet now.

Dad's Angelo spoke differently, stank of BO, smoked, drank beer and ate a clove of garlic every morning when he got up and every night before he went to bed. 'I've-ah nev-ah had-ah cold-ah in-ah my life-ah!'

'Yeah, but you make everyone round you wish they had one, so they wouldn't have to smell ya!' Both of them used to laugh when Dad said that.

When Gary lobbed onto Santa's knee that day, he said he wished he had a cold.

'That's pretty funny, kid,' said Santa. 'Play in the rain and I reckon you might just get one. Stick that in ya Santa sack, eh?' Then he gave Gary a lollipop, said,

'Smile, be good to your mum and dad' and pushed him off his knee and towards the door.

What a suck.

That Christmas, Gary tried to stay up to see the real Santa, so he could tell him what was going on with the department store Santa he'd seen that year. He knew it was dobbing, and no one really liked a dobber, but this was something the real Santa had to know about.

Gary watched his bedside clock tick over – past eight, then nine, ten and eleven. To keep himself awake he sang Christmas carols and straightened the Santa sack at the end of his bed. Gary was pretty sure he heard the town clock chime eleven-thirty, too. It was just one dong on the half-hour.

Santa would have to turn up soon, otherwise his sleigh would change into a pumpkin and the reindeer would – what? Not be reindeer? Gary was mixing up his stories again. Blow it. He knew that if he didn't get a grip he'd soon be asleep. And then suddenly he was. And he had a dream that Santa was really his mum. This totally freaked him out.

In the morning, young Gary woke to find that Santa had been and gone. The Santa sack was kind of full and the mince pie and milk that Gary had left out had been mauled. He knew he should have written Santa a note, instead of trying to wait up. Santa could have read it while he was stuffing himself. But

then, he might have choked on the pie if he'd heard how bad the department store Santa was.

Maybe Gary should have set a trap. He could have hung a net, or a shopping trolley, laid a trip-wire, rigged up a bell. But then, that might have ticked Santa off and made him decide not to leave any presents. And that would definitely have stunk like old fish.

The following Christmas Gary and his mum caught the train to town again, and this time Santa wasn't even a man. He was a woman dressed up as a man. Either that, or Santa had a ponytail, plucked eyebrows, a badly stuck-on beard and very large breasts.

Not good enough, thought Gary FJ Peterson. If this sort of thing kept happening, if Santa was represented so badly from year to year, maybe he would stop coming to Australia altogether. Who'd want to show his face in a country where the people pretending to be him barely even tried?

And what about later – at the end? Gary didn't really like to think about it, but he had to. Everyone did. It was one of life's big questions: up there with *How do we know we're alive?* and *If a tree falls in the forest and no one is there to hear it, does it make any noise?*

The question Gary kept coming back to was this: *When Santa died, eventually – not now, but one day – someone would have to replace him. And what would be the chance of the next Santa being an Aussie?* The answer he kept getting was *No chance at all.*

So sometime between sitting on Mrs Santa's lap and fifteen years ago, Gary decided he wanted to be the best Santa in Australia. Maybe even the world. And then, if he was as good as he thought he could be, and he was right about them eventually having to choose a new Santa, and all the planets lined up the right way and the stars shone down on him – well, he could be the one.

Gary could be Super Santa. One day. But he

knew that he had to start small. He couldn't just jump into the top job. He'd kick off as a Super(market) Santa. Then he could work his way up to a department store Santa, then a shopping mall Santa. A Supa-Centa Santa. A parade Santa, then a Carols by Candlelight Santa and then, maybe – if his hair turned pure white and his beard grew big and bushy and his gut was mostly out the front and not out the side – if all that happened and Santa died and they needed to replace him, well –

It made Gary sad to think about it, but he had to. He owed it to Santa.

They changed popes once in a while. Sometimes it was a very long while, but they still had to change them. To Gary, Santa was even holier than the pope, and certainly more important. He was Christmas. Santa was a faith that kids could hold onto all year long. There wasn't much else that made them want to be good.

What kid played up when Mum or Dad said, 'If you don't cool your jets Santa won't come, okay?' Not one!

Santa wasn't magic. He wasn't an elf and he wasn't a cartoon character or a movie star or a myth. Santa Claus, Father Christmas, FX. He was a man. A man who would one day need replacing. Not that Gary wished Santa dead. What an awful thought. It was just that if Santa did die, Gary would be there, ready to help out.

He was perfect for the job and the reason was as plain as the rather round nose on his face. Gary loved Father Christmas.

Or Gazza. That's what he'd get the elves to call him – just like the boys at the cricket club did when he used to play. 'Good one, Gazza!' they sang at him after a bag of wickets or a ton of runs. 'Beauty, Gaz!'

Gary FJ Peterson was ready to step up. He'd put a bit of Aussie twang into the 'Ho ho ho'. The world deserved it and he deserved the world. Gary would do anything to drive that sleigh.

He pulled the bathroom door closed again and looked at himself in the mirror.

Perfect.

He really was Santa. Or he would be.

'You ready?' said the boss through the closed bathroom door.

'Oh, ho ho! Ho-lmost there, young fella. Just parking the sleigh and watering the reindeer. It's hot for them down here, you know.'

'Yeah, righto, Gary,' said the boss. He was a Santa as well, but not cut from the same cloth as Gary. 'Whateveryareggon! But it's five to nine, mate. The queue's halfway up aisle three, it's past the dunny roll and heading for toothbrushes and the nappy products already. It's going to be a long day, mate.'

'Yeah, yeah. The reindeer aren't used to weather like this in December,' said Gary. 'Just one more minute.' He gave his beard a final brush, licked his fingers, twirled his eyebrows to match his moustache and winked. It was a long road, but it was a start. If Santa was a superhero, this was what he would look like.

'Go, Santa. Go!'

POOH, WHO FARTED?

Santa: Aha! Now I get it!

Gallery Guy: What do you get, Santa?

Santa: I've worked it out.

Gallery Guy: What have you worked out?

Santa: What they mean. I know what the statues mean.

Gallery Guy: Brilliant. But they don't mean anything. They're just statues.

Santa: You're wrong, look – (Santa pointing at the Thinker).

Santa: He's holding his nose and saying, "Pooh, who farted?"

Santa: And he's pointing over there, at someone. He's saying, "He did!"

Santa: And this guy's saying, let's get the pig!

THE MAGIC PUDDING

My mum's made a magic pudding.

It hasn't got legs, it can't talk, and it doesn't change into any dessert you want. And her pudding certainly doesn't speak. That's *the* magic pudding in this book I was reading.

But Mum's pudding is magic just the same.

She made it last Christmas. I think she was trying to be Grandma, who's always made puddings. They hang in her laundry cupboard all year like boxing bags, then she pulls them out on Christmas Day and steams up the whole house.

That'd be great if Grandma lived somewhere cold. She doesn't.

Grandpa always grumbles. He slaps the windows open and on the really hot days points at least two fans at the stove. It never helps. The place always steams up, because it's not very big.

This year, for the first time I can remember, we're having Christmas at our house, and that's why Mum made the pudding. I think she does fancy herself as a bit of a Grandma – at least, that's what Dad says when she drives.

She got all of us to stir the pudding and make a wish when we did it. This was very important. Mum says lots of things go into puddings. I saw sultanas and eggs and flour and even those disgusting bright red cherries that come in a plastic packet. They don't taste nearly as good as they look. She said other things go into puddings, but you can't see them. She was stirring away at the bench and said, 'A bit of love, a sprinkle of tenderness. Some magic, ooops, that's lots of Christmas magic. Friendship, family and good wishes to everyone.'

'Oh, spew,' I said. 'Any more of that stuff and we'll choke on it.'

'You're such a boy,' said Mum. 'I'll put an extra kiss in there, just for you.'

'Mum!' I moaned. I gave the pudding a stir with the spoon and made a wish. She said if I wanted the wish to come true I'd have to do it with my hands, so I stuck a finger in, closed one eye and had a quick wish; the kind you don't really think about. The soccer was on TV; time was running out for the Socceroos.

That night, Mum wrapped the mix up in a scungy old cloth and hung it in the laundry, just as Grandma did. And the only time I remembered it was when Mum said to get the vacuum cleaner, because the pudding lived in the same cupboard.

It was just like Grandma's pudding. It hung there like a speedball begging to be punched, so I gave it a few uppercuts.

Summer cooled to winter, which warmed to spring. By the time I'd got my cricket gear out from under the bed I knew we were getting closer to summer. Mum started hanging the pudding in front of the clothes drier. She was worried it had gone a bit squidgy. She had no idea I'd been giving it the odd whack.

On Christmas Day the relatives spilled out of their cars, wearing new clothes and old smiles. By the time they'd set all their presents under the tree, the corner of the living room looked like the foyer in a department store.

I love Christmas.

Grandma went for kisses first and the pudding second. She was in charge now. She'd brought her big copper pot to boil it in and moved everything off the stovetop, so she could get it happening. Grandpa asked if we had any fans.

I helped Dad bring the outside table in, then Mum and my sister fussed about setting the table. One green ribbon up one side, a red ribbon up the other.

There were enough places set for two cricket sides. And we'd play later, somehow. Our backyard was the home of six-and-out. I'd lost more balls than I could count in Mr Spilozia's yard, and he never threw them back. Old dog.

My sister was given a totem tennis set by Santa, so we had a tournament while the Turkey cooked. Dad said it was Wimbledon. By the time we got to the quarter-finals only my sister and the men were left. When Uncle Reg knocked Bella out, she cried.

Auntie Soph growled at Uncle Reg, who said Bella could take his place. But he never actually let go of the bat, so Bella skulked off and got into a game of something else with the cousins.

Dad won. He opened a bottle of champagne and sent the cork flying over Mr Spilozia's fence. 'Merry Christmas!' he yelled, while he sprayed the contents around the backyard and Mum called him a drongo.

The pudding bubbled away on the stove. The way the lid bounced was a bit like music.

We pulled the crackers, put on the daggy hats and told the jokes. They seemed even lamer this year than last.

'Knock knock.'
'Who's there?'
'Mary.'
'Mary who?'
'Mary Christmas.'

Everyone clapped when Dad set the turkey down on the table. All the men had an opinion on how to carve it and none of them held theirs back. There were a couple of crispy bacon rashers on top of it, so Dad knocked them off and asked if that was the right way to start.

Before anyone answered he sliced into the giant bird. 'Hmmm,' was all he said, but it was enough to get every adult eye at the table taking a closer look at what he was up to. He sliced into the other side, 'Hmmmm'd again, then said it might need another five or so minutes.

'Five or so *hours*! That bird's nowhere near cooked!' Mum was spewing.

Dad said he didn't understand. 'I put the thermometer in and it said it was cooked. Look.' He grabbed the steel rod off the bench and stabbed it into the turkey's leg. 'See?' The needle worked its way around the dial to DONE.

'You're supposed to stick it up the chook's khyber!' roared Uncle Reg.

'Reg,' miffed Auntie Elle.

'What's its khyber?' I said.

'The Khyber Pass,' said Reg, shouldering Dad out of the way and putting the thermometer up the turkey's bum. 'The Khyber Pass is the – '

'We get it, thanks, Reginald,' said Grandma.

The needle on the thermometer hung around RAW.

Dad put the bird back in the Weber, while Grandpa cut ham off the bone.

The leg of pork was perfect, but there wasn't enough crackling for everyone. Me, Mum, Dad and Bella had to go without.

Tinkle, bubble, tinkle went Mum's magic pudding.

In the end we didn't even need the turkey. It stayed in the barbecue for the rest of the day. When Dad finally remembered it, the poor bird was half the size it was the last time we'd all seen it. I stuck the thermometer in its bum and the needle spun right past DONE and off the dial.

Mum declared halftime on Christmas lunch.

Me, Bella and the cousins hung around the Christmas tree, shaking presents. My cousin Mikey told me what his family were giving me. *Oh, cool*, I thought. *Another home made calendar with pictures of your family. Just what I wanted. It's not as if a Shane Warne spin ball was what I was after.* But I knew Mum'd gush over it, just as she did every year, when Aunty Helen gave it to her. It didn't seem fair that we gave their family a present each and they gave us one present for the whole family.

The dads stayed at the table talking man talk and Powderfinger. Grandpa said they'd never be Neil Diamond or have a hot August night. To us they might as well have been talking in a foreign language. The mums were talking their own game in the kitchen. Up one end, plates were scraped then rinsed then washed. Mum and Grandma had the other end, where they wrestled the pudding out of the copper pot. When Grandma untied the string and peeled back the cloth, she gave her head a little shake and gave Mum a happy punch on the shoulder.

'That's my girl,' she said. 'It's magic, hon. A work of art.'

'It is, isn't it!' grinned Mum. She was the cat who had the cream. The other mums clapped, so the dads did, too.

When halftime was over, we were all back at the table with one of Dad's whistles. What were we – dogs? But then, we all came back when he did it, so maybe.

Grandma made the camera call and everyone disappeared again, but got back pretty smartly. No one wanted to miss the pudding shot. I had my phone. Two megapixels, but my photo would be better than anyone else's, because I'd be able to text it straight-away. Pretty cool. I looked around the table and saw all those smiling faces beaming behind their cameras. We were like paparazzi – only it was all about the pudding, so we were pudderazzi.

'Everyone ready?' said Mum.

'Born ready,' said Cousin Mikey. He had his phone out, too. But it was old. One megapixel at most. I bet he couldn't even message with that thing.

Mum tipped a cap of brandy on the pudding, but Grandma had the matches. She fumbled the first, then got it together with the second. The flame hit the pudding. *Fwooop!* A thin blue flame tried to make noise as it covered the rest of the pudding. The cameras flashed, everyone cheered and the flame went out.

We all checked our pictures. We were going to look like a table of monkeys, faces screwed up, scratching about with our cameras or phones. No wonder they called it 'chimping'. And not one of us caught the flame in our shots. It wasn't that much of a surprise, because every year the same thing happened.

It sometimes made me wonder if the flame was ever really there. 'I saw it,' Grandpa would say. 'It was there, all right.'

With great ceremony, Grandma passed Mum her special pudding knife. It only ever got a run on Christmas Day and only in Grandma's hands, so this was a moment. Mum looked as if she was going to tear up.

'*You've* got to slice your first pudding, hon,' Grandma gushed. 'It's only right.'

Mum took the knife and turned it slowly in her hands. The handle was red, and shaped like a line of berries. The blade was the colour of Grandma's hair, silver and yet sort of dull at the same time. But unlike Grandma's hair, it was thick. Words had been etched into the knife, along with pictures of Christmas. Holly. Reindeer. Santa. And snow that was melting from too many Christmases and puddings and too much washing up with Ajax, so it'd be clean and ready for next Christmas, too.

Mum rested the knife on the top of her pudding and closed her eyes.

Another wish.

When she opened her eyes she gave Grandma, then Grandpa the smallest smile. And they sent one back.

Then cousin Mikey started a chant. 'Pudding. Pudding. Pudding.' He added a slow handclap, as if he was in the outer at the cricket. All the kids joined in. We just wanted to get our mitts on the money. Every family pudding was stuffed with old fashioned pre-decimal coins – the ones you were allowed to use because they weren't poison. We'd pick our way through the first serve, hoping for a piece of hidden silver and have a second piece in the hope of more. Then we traded them in for money we could spend.

Threepence was worth twenty cents, sixpence got you fifty and anything else earned a whole a dollar.

Only the kids got paid.

'Pudding. Pudding. Pudding.' Now Uncle Reg stood up and conducted, using his spoon as a baton.

'You are a bogan,' said Uncle Pete.

'Which makes you this bogan's brother,' sang Uncle Reg in time with his spoon.

'Yeah, yeah!' Mum rose above the din. She laid the knife blade back on top of the pudding, and pushed.

'Pudding! Pudding! Pudding!'

Then she lifted the knife from the pudding and stared at it.

'Come on, Auntie Jo. It's payday. Let's go.' Cousin Mikey always found the most coins, even if that meant nicking them out of someone else's piece.

Mum gave him the look, and rattled her head in a way that said shut up without having to say it. Mikey didn't recognise it as Mum's shut-up look, so he kept on chanting.

'Pudding. Pudding. Pudding.'

Mum stuck her head forward and pulled her jaw back. It's not her best look, especially when she leaves her mouth open. She held Grandma's pudding knife above her magic pudding, pulled her head back and stabbed. The knife bounced back at her, as if it had hit something. There was a *clink*. Maybe it had hit a coin.

Up went the knife again.

'Careful,' Grandma said. But if Mum heard it, she didn't listen. She took another swipe at her pudding and again the knife jumped off its target. It was more what a cricket or boxing commentator might call a "glancing blow". I thought I'd like to be a commentator, so I tried to remember their weirder calls.

It was as if the knife actually bounced off Mum's magic pudding. There was no *boing* or *sploing* or cartoon noise. Just the squeal of Grandma's knife as it came off the pudding and into the table where it got a new bend in the blade.

Grandma squealed again.

Mum squealed, too.

Her pudding had slipped off the plate and was rolling across the table, leaving a trail of pudding squelch and burnt brandy. The brown line could have been anything. Pudding pooh. A snail trail.

'Don't touch it. It's hot!' yelled Mum. 'It's been in the cooker all bubbling day!'

The pudding rolled down the length of the table, the lines of red and green ribbons like tracks for it to follow. Nothing was safe. Mum's Magic Pudding roll-ed over glasses and cutlery and, just as it was heading past Uncle Reg, it took a right turn – straight for his lap. He jumped back in his chair, caught the ball on his left knee and sent it into the air.

'Hot,' he said. 'It's hot!'

The pudding came down, but he sent it back into the air with his right knee, and higher this time. Much higher. It was as if Uncle Reg was juggling a soccer ball. He'd played at uni however many years ago, and still managed to talk up his skills.

He kept one eye on the ball and another on the back door behind him. The door was open, of course, like anything else that could have been opened to let the kitchen heat out of the house. Uncle Reg pushed his seat right away from the table. The pudding was back in gravity's grip.

He rocked on his chair, and before the pudding was back at head height, he seemed to flip over on himself. A backwards seated cartwheel? A somersault? The greatest indoor soccer moment in our Christmas Day history? It was like something out of the highlights package from the World Cup. Uncle Reg had his hair slicked back and was tanned. He even looked a bit Brazilian.

The pudding flew off his foot with a *thwack*, through the open door and out to the backyard, where it bounced off the newly repotted and almost dead lemon tree, past the totem tennis set and right into the soccer net that was always set up at the northern end of the garden. I figured that was what the commentators would call it, even though I wasn't sure where it stood on the compass.

We couldn't believe it.

What a shot! And the pudding didn't burst or split or anything. It was magic.

Uncle Reg jumped up off the floor, pulled his shirt over his head and did a lap of the table, then the backyard. He had his arms out as if he was an aeroplane and yelled one long, continuous 'Scooooooooooooooooooooooore!' It was exactly like the World Cup.

I think the only reason he stopped was because he was out of breath, otherwise he might have run around forever. He had his hands on his knees and his gut wasn't far behind. 'I told you I could play, didn't I?' he puffed.

I raced out and got Mum's pudding from the back of the net. And now it was cool enough to handle.

Cousin Mikey charged outside and begged me to pass it to him.

'You'll just rip it open for the money,' I said. But he promised he wouldn't, so I kicked it to him and he kicked it back.

Mum's pudding looked like a dirty soccer ball. It was the same size and pretty much the same shape. Then Grandma came out and picked it up off the ground.

'Oh, Gran,' said Cousin Mikey.

'If I've told you once I've told you a thousand times, Michael, don't play with your food!' She picked up Mum's pudding and started flicking the grass off it. Then she squeezed it. She gave it a little toss in the air and caught it. Then she squeezed it again.

She looked at Mum. 'How did you make this?'

'The way you told me to,' said Mum. 'It's your recipe.'

Grandma put the pudding to her ear and shook it. 'What did you wish for when you were mixing it?'

Mum curled a lip and shook her head. Then Grandma looked at me.

I tried to remember what I'd wished for. It took a while, but when I did I decided that next year, I was going to wish for a new bike.

Or an Xbox.

Or a go-kart.

Or, ah, something better than a magic pudding.

Andrew   Terry

Hey you! Check out:

www.andrewdaddo.com.au

www.terrydenton.com

PHOTOS: These are old photos of Andrew and Terry at Christmas time! Have you noticed that whenever someone gets in trouble or dies and there's a report on the news, the only photos they have are awful and blurry . . . well, these are a bit like that.